Eyewitness Reliability in Motor Vehicle Crashes:
A Primer for Practitioners
Second Edition

Patrick J. Robins, Ph.D.

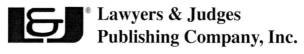
Lawyers & Judges Publishing Company, Inc.
Tucson, Arizona

This publication is designed to provide accurate and authoritative information in regard to the subject matter covered. It is sold with the understanding that the publisher is not engaged in rendering legal, accounting, or other professional service. If legal advice or other expert assistance is required, the services of a competent professional person should be sought.

—From a Declaration of Principles jointly adopted by
a Committee of the American Bar Association
and a Committee of Publishers and Associations.

The publisher, editors and authors must disclaim any liability, in whole or in part, arising from the information in this volume. The reader is urged to verify the reference material prior to any detrimental reliance thereupon. Since this material deals with legal, medical and engineering information, the reader is urged to consult with an appropriate licensed professional prior to taking any action that might involve any interpretation or application of information within the realm of a licensed professional practice.

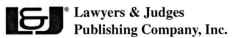 **Lawyers & Judges
Publishing Company, Inc.**

P.O. Box 30040 • Tucson, AZ 85751-0040
(800) 209-7109 • FAX (800) 330-8795
e-mail: sales@lawyersandjudges.com
www.lawyersandjudges.com

Library of Congress Cataloging-in-Publication Data

Robins, Patrick J.
  Eyewitness reliability in motor vehicle crashes : a primer for practitioners / Patrick J. Robins. -- 2nd ed.
      p. cm.
  Rev. ed. of: Eyewitness reliability in motor vehicle accident reconstruction and litigation. 2001
  Includes bibliographical references and index.
  ISBN-13: 978-1-933264-68-4 (softcover : alk. paper)
  ISBN-10: 1-933264-68-3 (softcover : alk. paper)
  1. Liability for traffic accidents. 2. Evidence (Law) 3. Witnesses. 4. Fallibility. 5. Traffic accident investigation. I. Robins, Patrick J. Eyewitness reliability in motor vehicle accident reconstruction and litigation. II. Title.
  K946.A8R63 2009
  347.73'66--dc22

2009018621

Printed in the United States of America
10 9 8 7 6 5 4 3 2 1

Dedication

To my wife Rosemary, and my children Kelly and Brenna, whose time with husband and father respectively was irretrievably stolen away by the many weeks spent lecturing and writing as this book took shape and during which they surely must have tasted, firsthand, the flavor of a single parent household.

Contents

Preface

I recently gave evidence at a criminal trial in which a young man was charged with dangerous driving. The young man had lost control of his vehicle which contained several passengers, resulting in crippling injuries to one of the occupants. I had determined the speed of the vehicle based on compelling physical evidence and presented this calculation at trial. During the cross examination, the prosecuting attorney and I engaged in the following exchange:

> Prosecutor: You will agree with me, sir, that people who are travelling in their vehicles beside or being overtaken by a vehicle which subsequently left road marks would be in a better position to estimate the accurate speed of the vehicle?
> A: No, I would not agree with that.
> Prosecutor: You are suggesting that by looking at a minimum, being road evidence, grass and gravel evidence, and then vaulting...that you're in a better position than somebody who is being overtaken by a vehicle to say how fast that vehicle was going?
> A: I would trust the physical evidence over the eyewitness testimony any day, any time.
> Prosecutor: So, if a person is doing 120 [km/h] and is passed by a vehicle and that person who is the person doing the passing subsequently says they were doing—or the road evidence says they were doing 109 [km/h], you would disbelieve the person who says they were being overtaken at 120 [km/h]?
> A. I would.

In hindsight, I somewhat regretted my "any day, any time" statement as being a bit too encompassing, but it represented a culmination of sentiment that grew from years of training and experience within both the psychology and collision reconstruction fields. It was clear from the prosecutor's line of questioning that within the legal community a powerful penchant for eyewitness evidence still exists today. Almost reflexively, I responded under pressure to an urge to set the record straight, to cry out to anyone within earshot that the physical evidence, if it exists, ought to be the driving impetus toward the truth of the case. The continuing preference for human evidence over physical evidence requires a solid faith in eyewitness testimony, one which is perhaps most simply stated by Ainsworth (1998) when he wrote, "judges and juries are still accepting the evidence of eyewitnesses as though such testimony were an objective, factual and indisputable truth" (p. 2).

The idea that eyewitnesses might be mistaken is not a new idea; scientific concern with the reliability of witnesses and the fallibility of human memory can be traced back several decades. This book has been taking shape in my mind for several years now. The need for it became evident when I began to combine my formal training in psychology and in collision reconstruction with experience gained from actual collision reconstruction work. The focus of the book was guided by a continuing series of lectures that I have given about human factors in collision reconstruction, owing in great part to the germinal work of Elizabeth Loftus and her colleagues in the 1970s. The motivating force behind this book stemmed from my growing impatience with the legal community and its reluctance to fully embrace the power of physical evidence, as well as its reluctance to release or at least substantially relax its grip on eyewitness testimony as the ultimate lever of truth in collision reconstruction cases.

This book is not particularly aimed at scholars in the area of eyewitness reliability. Rather, it is aimed at working practitioners within the broad field of collision reconstruction and might include at the very least reconstructionists, lawyers, judges, police officers, engineers, insurance investigators, and researchers. The book is intended as a brief primer to guide these individuals through the onerous task of sorting out the relative importance of physical and human evidence in collision reconstruction work. This book is not intended as a review of the massive body of scholarly work in the area of eyewitness reliability, a body of work which continues to grow annually. As specific lines of research from the scientific community bear on a particular aspect of collision reconstruction, they will be introduced.

Chapter 1 of this book sets the stage for the inevitable legal contest that frequently pits physical evidence against human evidence. It introduces the reader to the respective roles of these two kinds of evidence in the field of collision reconstruction. Chapters 2, 3, and 4 guide the reader through much of what we presently understand about human perception, memory, and forgetting, demonstrating along the way the fragility of human recollection. Chapter 5 discusses the relationship between the world of scientific research in the area of eyewitness reliability and the practical real world. Finally, Chapter 6 summarizes the principal findings and looks to the future with respect to eyewitness reliability and collision reconstruction.

I hope that in reading this book you will be struck by the simultaneous power and frailty of human perception and human memory. I hope to demonstrate the need to foster a healthy skepticism regarding eyewitness evidence within the legal and collision reconstruction communities. Finally, I hope to inspire a new appreciation for the value of physical evidence in reconstructing motor vehicle collisions.

Chapter 1

Physical Evidence versus Human Evidence: What's the Big Deal Here Anyway?

Synopsis

The field of motor vehicle collision reconstruction is broad and multidisciplinary in nature. The ultimate goal of any collision investigation is to gain an understanding of why a particular collision occurred. This understanding can later be put to a variety of uses. A police officer might use this understanding to lay charges; an engineer might use it as a basis for redesigning a roadway; or, a lawyer might use this understanding to support a client's claim in a criminal or civil action. While the final utility of an investigation's results will vary with the user, the general goal remains the same: to determine and describe the sequence of events leading up to and culminating in a collision. The events of interest might be mechanical in nature, such as the dynamics of a skidding vehicle or the kinematics of an ejected occupant, or they might be human, as in the thoughts and actions of a driver. Thus, the field of collision reconstruction borrows from a variety of disciplines, including but not necessarily limited to physics, engineering, psychology, biomechanics, and medicine.

In any field of inquiry over time, specialization of interest and expertise is inevitable, and the field of collision reconstruction is no exception. Nonetheless, all reconstructionists, regardless of their particular interests, share the need for accurate information. At the core, there are really only two sources of information about the events of a particular collision, *physical evidence* and *human evidence*.

Physical evidence consists of traces left by the involved vehicles, people, and objects during the collision events. Tire marks, collision fluids and debris, damaged vehicles and property, human bodies, fluids, and tissue all constitute physical evidence.

Human evidence consists of recollections of the events of a collision held by drivers, occupants, and bystanders. Human evidence is the final product of a variety of human processes, beginning with an observation or action by an individual and ending with a formal statement that reflects, at a particular point in time, the recollection of that observation or action.

Collision investigators and reconstructionists make use of both physical and human evidence in their work. The respective uses and limitations of each type of evidence will be discussed separately below.

1.1 Making Use of Physical Evidence

Physical evidence defines the presence, at some unique point in time, of an object of interest in the collision investigation. A tire mark on the roadway, for example, indicates the tire's location in the driving environment at some time during the collision. A clump of hair in a shattered windshield indicates the space a passenger's head occupied at the point in time at which the head contacted the windshield. A black rubber transfer on the side of a vehicle might define where a particular tire contacted another vehicle at some point in time during the impact between two vehicles.

Three to four centuries ago, Galileo's observations and Newton's synthesis of them established a framework for our understanding of the motion of objects in the universe that persists today. This framework forms the foundation for interpreting much of the physical evidence that we encounter at the scene of a collision. While occasionally a new measurement procedure or a new application of one of the basic laws of motion is introduced into the collision reconstruction field, the principles themselves remain intact. Collision reconstructionists rely on physical evidence and fundamental natural laws, such as Newton's laws of motion, to determine the time, distance, and velocity relationships between interacting and colliding objects.

Physical traces at the scene of a motor vehicle collision often provide irrefutable evidence of how the collision occurred. The nature and length of tire marks may provide evidence of the direction of travel or speed of a vehicle. Human body tissue and fluids may provide evidence of contact points between vehicles and occupants or between vehicles and pedestrians. Such evidence is a natural outcome of physical laws. These laws are uniformly accepted as correctly describing the motion of bodies anywhere in the known universe, provided that the bodies are not travelling at or near the speed of light (299,338 kilometers per second or 186,000 miles per second), which appears to be a fairly reasonable assumption for earthbound vehicles. It is these very laws and their causal relationships with collision objects that are used by collision investigators to reconstruct the vehicle dynamics and occupant kinematics in a given collision.

Each year in the United States, at such institutions as the University of North Florida's Institute of Police Technology and Management, the Engineering Extension Services at Texas A&M University, and the Traffic Institute at Northwestern University, a large number of police officers and engineers receive training designed to enable them to apply basic principles in physics to the reconstruction of motor vehicle crashes.

1.2 Limitations of Physical Evidence

Physical evidence is certainly subject to degradation from natural forces over time: tire marks may fade due to weathering and traffic wear; fluids and debris may be altered or moved; occupants may move or be removed and vehicle and property damage may be repaired. For the most part, the degradation of physical evidence is predictable and relatively slow. Procedures can be developed or adopted that permit the documentation of such evidence prior to its inevitable debasement. Additionally, much physical evidence can be photographically or otherwise preserved for future examination and analysis.

But, not all collision events leave physical traces. Some, such as a driver's pre-collision thoughts or perceptions will leave no physical evidence. Some, such as a driver's actions, may only be inferred from other existing pieces of physical evidence, but do not themselves constitute physical evidence. Yet, a driver's perceptions and actions may be critical events leading up to a collision. Without accurate descriptions of these, a full understanding of the collision may not be gleaned. While the motion of the vehicles, occupants, and objects involved in a collision are easily described by laws of physics, the complex interaction of factors precipitating the collision are not likely to be so easily described.

Imagine a vehicle which has encountered a slippery section of road and slides uncontrollably off the roadway, down an embankment and into a tree. The loss of control and the resultant path that the vehicle takes can be understood by an analysis of vehicle dynamics. The speed of the vehicle at the point at which control is lost and at impact with the tree might be discovered in the same manner. The motion of the occupants inside the vehicle and their resultant injuries might be ascertained in like fashion. Can the cause of this collision be fully understood by such knowledge? Why did this particular vehicle experience a loss of control at this particular moment? Why didn't other vehicles that came before it experience the same outcome? How was this particular vehicle and its occupants different from all the other similar vehicles that traveled the same stretch of roadway at about the same time but did so without incident? Why did this driver lose control of this vehicle?

These questions prompt us to consider that collision reconstruction is not a simple matter because collisions are the product of a series of related events in which driver, vehicle, and roadway interact dynamically over time; a change in any one of the three can produce an entirely different outcome. No two real-world collisions are the same. Each is a unique sequence of occurrences in which the participants act, react, and alter the future course of events by doing so. To attempt to understand a collision, without considering the characteristics of the participants, would be a futile exercise. The search for cause necessarily demands that we examine events preceding the impact itself.

To understand why a collision occurs, we must examine the human evidence, beginning as far back in time as is necessary to fully explain the chain of events that we are investigating.

1.3 Making Use of Human Evidence

Human evidence consists primarily of witness statements from drivers, occupants, and bystanders pertaining to their recollected observations of the collision. Witness statements are routinely gathered as part of a collision investigation, and these statements form part of the working file. Human evidence provides a window through which to examine those events that do not leave physical traces.

Imagine arriving at the scene of a collision in which two vehicles have collided at right angles within an intersection. Both drivers claim that the traffic signal showed green for their respective directions of travel. While physical evidence gathered at the scene might enable the investigator to determine the direction of travel of each vehicle, the speeds of the vehicles, the location of impact, and any pre-collision braking of the vehicles, it could not determine right-of-way in this case; here we must turn to human evidence. Statements provided by the drivers, other motorists, occupants, and bystanders would all constitute the human evidence that might be required to address the issue of right-of-way in this collision.

There are, of course, many situations in which critical collision issues can only be addressed through human evidence. Human evidence can be a powerful weapon in the reconstructionist's arsenal, but as with all powerful weapons, it must be used with appropriate safeguards and cautions.

1.4 Limitations of Human Evidence

Human evidence reflects the recollected observations and actions of an individual at a particular point in time relative to the collision itself. Between the time of the witness's initial observation or action and the time that he or she gives a formal statement, many processes may have acted on the recollection. Even the observation itself is an individual interpretation of an event in the real world, a personal perception that is equally subject to many influences. Human evidence, in contrast to physical evidence, is much more dynamic. While we tend to view our recollections as relatively stable and independent of worldly influence, the empirical evidence available suggests that they are anything but. We operate under the myth that our recollections of collision events, once observed, are relatively permanent and unerring in nature. Buckout (1984) described this phenomenon as follows:

> Uncritical acceptance of eyewitness testimony seems to be based on the fallacious notion that the human observer is a perfect recording device that everything that passes before his or her eyes is recorded and can be "pulled out" by sharp questioning or "refreshing one's memory". In a categorical statement, which psychologists rarely make, I argue that this is impossible—human perception and memory function effectively by being selective. A human being has no particular need for perfect recall, perception and memory are decision-making processes affected by the totality of a person's abilities, background, environment, attitudes, motives, and beliefs, and by the methods used in testing recollection of people and events. (p. 211)

Human information processing and memory are dynamic processes that enable us to successfully adapt to ever changing circumstances. Buckout's sentiments are more recently echoed by Ainsworth (1998):

> Even the most honest and upstanding of witnesses will inevitably produce their own subjective and personal version of "the truth"... human perception and memory are not literal and objective recorders of "fact". Rather these processes are personalized and subjective interpreters and recorders of information....Is it reasonable to expect a witness to tell "the whole truth"? Such an expectation assumes

that witnesses are capable of taking in every small detail of the scene which they witnessed, and of storing these details accurately and fully. But surely this is naive and unrealistic? Humans are simply incapable of taking in all the information which they encounter. Perception is selective in what it attends to, and large amounts of detail simply go unnoticed. (pp. 2–3)

1.5 Evidence and Truth

The goal of any collision investigation is to arrive at a truthful picture of the events leading to the collision, but in collision reconstruction, truth can be elusive. The physical evidence may suggest one series of events while the human evidence suggests another. One hopes, of course, that the two go hand-in-hand, each supporting the other, but this is not always so. In 1999 the U.S. Department of Justice published a national guide for collecting and preserving human evidence entitled *Eyewitness Evidence: A Guide for Law Enforcement*. In this document appears a message from U.S. Attorney General, Janet Reno, in which she makes the following observations:

> Eyewitnesses frequently play a vital role in uncovering the truth about a crime. The evidence they provide can be critical in identifying, charging, and ultimately convicting suspected criminals. That is why it is absolutely essential that eyewitness evidence be accurate and reliable.... Recent cases in which DNA evidence has been used to exonerate individuals convicted primarily on the basis of eyewitness testimony have shown us that eyewitness evidence is not infallible. Even the most honest and objective people can make mistakes in recalling and interpreting a witnessed event; it is the nature of human memory. (p. iii)

This statement reflects a compelling recognition that human evidence must be viewed with caution in a legal context—a warning bell that psychologists have been sounding with increasing vigor since the 1970s. When eyewitness testimony alone or in substantial part represents the evidence of a particular case, then the danger posed by the potential fallibility of human recollection is most abundantly clear.

When both human and physical evidence exist, as is often the case in the field of collision reconstruction, is the same level of concern for eyewitness testimony still warranted? According to Loftus (1996) the answer is yes:

> [J]urors give eyewitness testimony much more weight than other sorts of evidence when reaching a verdict....All the evidence points

rather strikingly to the conclusion that there is almost nothing more convincing than a live human being who takes the stand, points a finger at the defendant, and says "That's the one!" (pp. 10–11)

In the preface of this book I presented a verbal exchange from a trial in which it was clear that a strong inclination still exists in our courts today toward human evidence over physical evidence.

It seems paradoxical that there should exist, within any judicial system, a preference for eyewitness testimony over physical evidence, but when placed within a human context this state of affairs can be viewed as quite natural. This neither surprises nor troubles me as a psychologist, but as a reconstructionist seeking to accurately describe a collision I find it quite frustrating at times. How do we account for this situation?

The application of physical laws, such as Newton's laws of motion, to collision reconstruction may not be intuitively obvious to triers of fact in the courtroom. It may even discourage acceptance by such individuals with its technical nature. This is not to say that jury members and judges are not capable of grasping the significance of the laws and mathematical equations that frequently accompany a collision reconstruction. It is perhaps more a matter of familiarity than of capability. People, all other things being equal, prefer that which is familiar to that which is not. The seemingly intuitive and familiar nature of personal testimony encourages its acceptance. Most people are reasonably confident in their abilities to judge the credibility of others and in their knowledge of the processes of human observation. After all, surely all but the youngest of us are experienced observers of the world and people around us. Most people are not, however, reasonably confident in their abilities to judge the application of physics and mathematics to the motions of vehicles.

Most reconstructionists have spent hundreds of hours in the classroom and in the field studying the underlying physics and mathematics essential for their craft. While it may be apparent to them that physical laws govern the motions of vehicles, it may be unrealistic to expect triers of fact to automatically subscribe to the same assumptions. When Newton formalized the laws of motion, he surely used as examples of moving bodies those objects that were familiar at the time. Clearly, these objects could not have included motorized vehicles. While many of us have encountered Newton's laws in high school, usually applied to bullets, balls, and planets, we may not regard the transition from such objects to vehicles as intuitive. Newton did not limit the application of the laws of motion to bullets and balls and planets; he regarded them as applying to all moving bodies in the known universe.

This is accepted as a universal truth, but while such things as cars, trucks, bicycles and buses, no less than bullets, balls, and planets may obey the same set of natural laws, such universal truths as the laws of mechanics may not be as readily accepted by triers of fact as they are by the scientific community. This may, in part, explain why triers of fact are more inclined to embrace human evidence.

The trier of fact, in hearing human evidence, faces the much simpler task of judging primarily whether the witness is credible or not. If he or she is judged as credible, then the recollections recounted by the witness ought to be believed. If the witness is judged as not credible, then the information ought to be dismissed. Of course, we neither expect nor desire that triers of fact have scientific expertise in collision reconstruction cases, but given that they usually do not, we must recognize that they might feel more comfortable dealing with human evidence than with physical evidence.

1.6 The Frailty of Human Evidence

Human evidence is a recollected series of events stated by a participant or bystander regarding a collision of interest. It is governed not by the natural laws of physics but by human thought processes. It is described not by mathematical equations but by the principles of biology and psychology. Human sensation, perception, and memory are the stuff of human evidence. To properly realize the role and value of eyewitness evidence in the field of collision reconstruction requires an understanding of how people perceive and remember what they experience.

Human evidence is accorded tremendous weight in our courts. Yet it is strikingly ironic that most collision investigators have little to no formal training on the fallibility of human observation. The following two chapters describe how individuals process information in the world around them and why our abilities to perceive and remember the details of a collision might be inadequate for the task.

Chapter 2

How We Process the World Around Us: What You See Is Not Necessarily What You Get

---

I am frequently awestruck, as I am sure most people are, at the extraordinary abilities of the human nervous system to process and store information. Imagine if you had the task of writing down everything you know; there would scarcely be enough paper and ink in the entire world to record it all. Yet, as powerful as these abilities are, the speed and capacity requirements for capturing the events of a collision far exceed normal human capability. A motor vehicle collision is a short lived event, lasting perhaps 100 milliseconds or so from first touch of the vehicles to their separation and movement toward final rest. In this chapter we will explore the limitations of human perceptual processes as they relate to our ability to observe motor vehicle collisions.

2.1 Sensation

Our awareness of the world around us begins with the process of sensation, in which stimuli, such as sights and sounds impinge upon our sense organs, in this case our eyes or ears, producing chemical changes in our nervous systems which can be interpreted and stored by our brains. While all of our senses are important, some are more critical in a driving context than others. The bulk of the information that we process while driving is visual, so we most importantly need to see what is happening. Hearing plays a less important, but not inconsequential, role. We often rely on sound to help us identify an important stimulus in our visual fields. Tactile experiences can be important, particularly with respect to sensing the forces of a vehicle in motion as we attempt to change direction or speed. Taste and smell are not normally vital to the successful operation of a motor vehicle, though they may, on occasion, alert us to potential danger as in the case of a vehicle fire. In order to appreciate the inherent limitations of our senses we must first understand how human sensory processes operate. The primary focus of this chapter will be on vision since its role for both the driver and observer are obvious.

2.2 How We See Anything

Successful operation of a motor vehicle involves seeing where the vehicle is in space relative to other objects in the environment, and maintaining the desired relative position of the vehicle at all times. This is made difficult by the fact that the vehicle is usually moving. Adding to this difficulty is the fact that many objects in the environment are also moving. This combination of moving vehicle and changing environment produces a very complex visual task for the driver.

To see anything around us in sufficient detail to recognize and identify it, three ingredients are required: (1) the target must be viewed foveally or centrally in our visual fields; (2) the target must have sufficient contrast to be distinguished from its background; and (3) the target must capture the attention. We will consider each of these requirements after a brief general discussion of the structure of the eye.

2.3 The Structure of the Eye

The human eye (see Figure 2.1) is a roughly spherical organ that captures and processes light. Light is allowed to enter through an opening in front called the *pupil*. The pupil is covered by a tough, curved membrane called the *cornea*. The cornea, in addition to protecting the inner eye from foreign material, provides most of the initial bending of the light rays that enter by virtue of its curved wet surface. The amount of light entering the eye is controlled by the diameter of the pupil. The *iris*, the coloured part of the eye, is the muscular machinery that dilates (opens) and constricts (closes) the pupil. Located just behind the pupil and controlled by its own set of muscles, the *ciliary muscles,* is the *lens.* The lens, by bulging or thinning in the middle, provides the remaining bending of the incoming light required to focus an image on the back wall of the eye, the *retina.* As we change focus from far objects to near objects and then back again, the lens correspondingly bulges for near focus (more light bending) and then thins out again (less bending) for distant focus.

The retina contains the light sensitive *photoreceptor cells* called the *rods* and *cones.* Their function is primarily to react chemically to light. Although rods and cones all react to light, they differ in number, location and specific sensitivity. Cones are concentrated primarily in the central portion of the retina (the *fovea*) while the more plentiful rods (about 20 times more) dominate the periphery and are absent in the fovea. The rods are much more sensitive to light. Under ideal viewing conditions a single candle's worth of light at a distance of 17 miles (27 km) is sufficient to stimulate the rods in the human eye. The cones, while dramatically less sensitive to light, are wavelength specific and confer colour perception, a feat not possible with rods alone. Additionally, cones by the manner in which they are connected to the brain in the neural fabric yield significantly greater acuity. Simply stated, rods are our nighttime photoreceptor (*scotopic* vision) cells and cones are our daytime (*photopic* vision) cells.

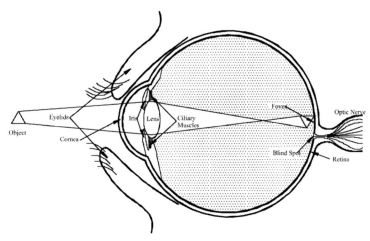

Figure 2.1 *Schematic diagram of the human eye.*

When light enters the eye and is focused on some part of the retina, the cells that receive that light respond by undergoing a chemical change. That chemical change is transmitted to the brain which results in a subjective experience that we know as a visual image. The nature and properties of the subjective image depend on where on the retina that light is focused and what type and number of cells are responding. Light from objects focused on the foveally located cones produce images that are clear, sharp, highly detailed and colourful. Light from objects that are focused on more peripheral regions of the retina yield images that are less distinct, less intense, less detailed and less colourful. As a target is viewed progressively farther out in the periphery of the visual field, it makes greater use of rods and lesser use of cones and is therefore seen as a less distinct or "fuzzier" image.

Both rods and cones, if continually stimulated, become fatigued, causing vision to fade. This fatigue is normally avoided by continually moving the eyes, thus varying the particular photoreceptor cells which are active at any one time. You can demonstrate this fatigue by very carefully, but firmly, pressing in on the outside edges of your eyelids with your fingers to prevent your eyeballs from moving. Within a few seconds, everything will fade to black as the receptor cells that are active become fatigued.

No photoreceptors exist where the *optic nerve*, which carries the information from the eyes to the brain, leaves the eye. This leaves a blind spot in the field of vision (See Figure 2.2.).

We are not normally aware of this blind spot because the brain fills in the missing information based on the data from other parts of the retina and from the other eye. As the eyes move, we develop clear images from the fovea, and the brain retains that information. This means that even though most of our visual field is fuzzy, the brain stores those clear images. Of course, subtle changes in those peripheral objects would not be detected until we actually refocused on them.

L   R

Figure 2.2 To experience your visual blind spot, hold the page about a foot away, close your right eye, and stare at the **R** on the right. Now slowly move the page closer until the **L** on the left disappears. At this point the left **L** is focused on your blind spot.

It is also interesting to note that the image of an object cast on the retina is actually upside down. In Figure 2.1, the object, a triangle, is oriented with the point facing up. The image on the retina has the point facing down. The brain processes the visual information and correctly interprets the world automatically.

2.4 Central Viewing versus Peripheral Viewing

The human field of view is fairly large, about 180 degrees from side to side and slightly less from top to bottom but the ability to discern detail is not uniformly distributed throughout this field. To see an object in detail it must be focused on a very small central portion of the retina, the fovea. This tiny area, densely packed with cone cells translates into a visual arc in our field of vision which is only about 2 to 3 degrees across, perhaps the size of a quarter dollar coin held at arm's length. Here our vision is most acute and we can see objects in colour and in great detail. As a target is focused farther away from this central region, the amount of detail drops off rapidly as the transition from cones to rods progresses. At an angle of only about 10 degrees away from the fovea, the acuity of an image drops off by 50% and at an angle of about 25 degrees, acuity is only about 10% when compared to foveal acuity. This rapid loss of detail in the periphery means that to see an object clearly we must look directly at it. For this reason the human eyes are constantly in motion, scanning back and forth, up and down, so that different parts of the field of view can be sampled in detail.

Objects in the periphery which are moving or flashing or particularly bright may capture our attention, thus causing us to look in their direction, focus them foveally and reveal the detail necessary to identify and process them.

How is it that the world appears to us to be clear and in focus if most of our visual field falls outside the area processed at the fovea? The answer, in part, lies in the fact that under normal conditions the eyes are in constant motion. Thus, different parts of the visual field are falling on the foveal area of the retina. The other part of the answer lies in the fact that our perception of the visual world is really a product of the brain, not the eyes.

2.5 The Role of Contrast

Even when we look directly at an object we will see it only if it stands out from the background against which it is being viewed. The set of properties inherent in an object that distinguish it from its background are known collectively as *contrast*. Contrast can be achieved in a number of ways, including brightness (light intensity), colour or hue, texture, size, shape or motion. An object which is considerably brighter or considerably dimmer than its background, for example, will be seen more readily. In the case that the object is dimmer than the background, it will be viewed as a silhouette. Camouflage is achieved by minimizing contrast, thus making it difficult to distinguish an object from its background and thus rendering it invisible.

The greater the contrast of an object, the more readily it will be seen or the more *conspicuous* it will be. The lower the contrast of an object, the more difficult it will be to see. A dark clad pedestrian on an unlit roadway at night, for example, is generally a fairly inconspicuous target since s(he) has very low contrast against a dark roadway and dark horizon, until being eventually illuminated by the vehicle's headlamps.

2.6 The Role of Attention

Even when an object is viewed centrally and has high contrast, it may still go unnoticed if a motorist's attention is focused on something else specifically. This phenomenon is known as *inattentional blindness*, a term coined by Mack and Rock (1998) and is often demonstrated by a videotaped exercise developed by Simons and Chabris (1999). In this exercise the subject views two teams (white shirts vs. black shirts) who are passing and dribbling basketballs and is asked to focus on just one team, the white shirts, and count the number of times that the ball changes hands amongst the players. When an unexpected and highly unusual target is introduced during this exercise (a person dressed in a gorilla costume walks on, stands facing the viewer directly beating her chest and then walks off), it usually goes unnoticed by most first-time viewers.

When we are thoroughly engaged in the visual processing of one event, other important events, most especially unexpected events, may go completely unnoticed, even though the images of those other events appear on the retinas of the eyes. We don't see everything that is before us; we see some things, those that we perceive to be important at the time, to the detriment of the others. It is critical to understand that **we see with our brains, not with our eyes** and even though the reflected light from an object might enter the eyes it will not necessarily be seen by us.

For a motorist to see anything in the roadway environment and recognize what it is, it must first capture his or her attention, be viewed centrally and have sufficient contrast to be distinguished from its background.

2.7 Day versus Night

The total range of light over which humans can see is enormous, from about 0.000003 lux to about 300,000 lux. As a reference, 1 lux is the amount of light falling on 1 square metre (about 10.75 square feet) of a surface from a single candle held at a distance of 1 metre (about 3.28 feet). To see over this range, however, it is necessary for the eyes to adapt to the changing level of light and this does not occur instantaneously. Through changes in pupil size (relatively quick) as well as changes to the photoreceptor cells and to the nervous system (relatively slow), we are able to gradually adapt to levels of light in this broad range. At the top of this range we function on cone vision alone and at the bottom of the range on rod vision alone. Daytime vision, by virtue of involving cone cells carries with it the greatest acuity. Nighttime vision, by contrast generally possesses lower levels of acuity, particularly as light levels drop low enough to require the more sensitive rod cells to become active.

At night, urban areas are usually lit artificially, partly from residential, public and commercial lighting, partly from fixed street lighting and partly from reflection of these sources of light off cloud cover. Additionally of course, vehicles carry sources of light with them in the form of head lamps, tail lamps and running lights. Consequently, driving at night uses both rods and cones (*mesopic* vision).

2.8 Adapting to Changing Light Conditions

Complete dark adaptation requires about 30 minutes or more. Because rods and cones are differentially sensitive to light, they adapt differently. Cone adaptation is complete within about 10 minutes which means that during adaptation, for the first short while, we see better in the central portion of the visual field. Our ability to see in the periphery steadily improves well after cone adaptation is complete. During the adaptation period any stray sources of light such as that from oncoming vehicles or changing ambient intensities can interfere with the ongoing adaptation and will complicate the process.

Once adaptation is complete, in sufficiently dark settings objects may be visible in the periphery but not in the central portion. Very dim objects, faint stars for example, are best viewed indirectly so that they activate rod cells. You may have had the experience of noticing a glimmer of light from a faint star off to the side in your visual field, only to have it disappear completely when you looked directly at it but return again when you once again looked away. In such a case the incoming light is insufficient to activate the cones in the fovea so the fovea may be essentially blind to these objects.

A pedestrian and motorist in a rural setting may not see what is outside of the vehicle's headlight beam in the same way. The pedestrians eyes will have adapted to whatever level of natural light exists, starlight and moonlight for example, whereas the motorist eyes will have adapted to the higher intensity of the headlamps of the vehicle as viewed through the glass of the vehicle. The pedestrian's eyes therefore may be considerably more sensitive to what lays beyond the reach of the headlamps than the driver, who will have adapted to the much brighter headlamps and therefore be less sensitive to dimmer sources. To obtain a sense of what might be visible to a driver, it is necessary, therefore, for the investigator to consider the view from inside the vehicle.

In like fashion, a driver and passenger may, by virtue of looking at different locations outside the vehicle at night and possibly through different types of glass, develop different sensitivities to the darker portions of the roadside environment. Just because a passenger saw something outside the vehicle does not necessarily mean that the driver ought to have done the same; passenger and driver may have developed different light sensitivities depending on where they had been looking.

Because urban centres have so many sources of light of various intensities at night, they present a challenge to the human visual system. As moving motorists experience different light intensities in different locations, the driver's eyes are adapting continuously to whatever intensity of light makes it through the glass of the vehicle to his or her eyes at a particular time. These levels of light may be significantly different from those for a stationary observer.

As people age, dark adaptation takes longer to achieve. Older drivers could therefore be at greater visual risk in urban settings at night where they might be required to adapt continuously to changes in light intensities from one locale to another.

2.9 Illuminance, Luminance and Things That Go Bump In the Night

Illuminance refers to the amount of light striking a surface, independent of an observer and of the reflective property of the surface. Depending on the intensity of the headlamps of a vehicle a certain amount of light will strike a target (illuminance). Some of that light may be absorbed and some of it may be reflected to the eyes of an observer, a driver for example. How much light is reflected from the target to the driver's or witness's eyes will depend on how reflective the surface is and the angle at which the reflected light is being viewed. The intensity of the reflected light reaching the observer's eyes is referred to as the *luminance* of the target. The apparent brightness of the target to the observer will depend on the target's luminance as well as on the target's contrast with the background and the ambient lighting conditions.

We see objects, day or night, by reflected light. Since daytime light intensities are so large, target luminance and reflectance are seldom a problem. At night, however, as light levels fall, the reflectance properties of the target become much more important. Clothing worn by a pedestrian, for example, can have a dramatic impact on the amount of light reflected off the pedestrian to an observer's eyes. Ambient street lighting can augment the headlamp-produced light falling on a target and alter the overall brightness of the target.

In rural settings, a vehicle's headlamps are the primary illuminating source of light and our ability to see a target will rely heavily on the intensity of the headlights at all distances. In urban settings, the vehicle's headlamps may be more or less significant depending on the overall street lighting levels and vehicle distances. At great distance, when the illuminating capability of headlights is lower, street lighting or other ambient lighting may play a more significant role. At closer distances, the vehicle headlamps may outshine the ambient lighting at the scene.

During the day, a number of factors play a role in a driver's ability to see and react to a target, many of which are attributable to or under the control of the driver:

- Contrast of the target
- Driver's visual focus
- Driver's focus of attention
- Driver's visual capabilities
- Driver's line-of-sight
- Condition of the vehicle glass surfaces
- Driver's perception-reaction time

At night the same factors as during the day impact on the ability of a motorist to see a target, but in addition, there are others, many of which are outside of the control of the driver:

- Reflectance properties of the target
- Intensity and aim of the vehicle's headlights
- Position of the target with respect to the primary light sources
- Glare from other light sources such as opposing headlights
- Scattering of light by inclement weather and vehicle glass
- Presence or absence of point sources of light carried by the target

2.10 Sensation versus Perception

The sensory organs of the human body collect stimuli from their surroundings and convert those stimuli into signals that can be transmitted and processed by the nervous system, which includes the brain. If we look at the human eye as an example, then light is the stimulus. The transformation from a stimulus, light in this case, to electrochemical events in the nervous system is referred to as *transduction* and the whole event is called *sensation*. Sensation ends when the stimulus of interest, a sight, sound, smell, taste, or feeling, is processed by the corresponding organ and coded in the nervous system, ready for interpretation by the brain. *Perception* refers to the subjective experience that we have when the brain selects, organizes, and interprets a particular sensation. Perception is really a product of the brain, while sensation is a product of the sensory organs.

Three examples come to mind that illustrate the variety of differences between sensation and perception. People who have lost limbs, for example, often report tingling, pain, and other sensations where the missing limbs used to be. This experience is referred to as the *phantom limb phenomenon*. Since all the tactile receptors attached to the missing limb are gone, no sensation is possible. The brain is still producing a perception that the limb is attached and able to feel, yet no sensory information is transmitted from the missing limb. In another related example, recall a vivid dream in which you were able to see, hear, and touch things as though they were real. No sensation of those things was actually being processed by the corresponding sensory organs during sleep, although they seemed real. The third example comes from the dentist's chair. Here we may experience a flood of sensation as the drill bit carves its path through our teeth, yet by blocking the signals from the teeth to the brain with an anaesthetic we eliminate the perception of pain. If the brain does not process the information from our senses then there is no perception of the experience, no conscious awareness of the event. This is important, and I will return to it later when I discuss memory.

Normally, sensation and perception work cooperatively. Our senses take in information about the world and code that information in the nervous system (sensation). That information is selected, organized and interpreted by the brain (perception). We then act on those perceptions. We can conveniently refer to this entire process as information processing.

2.11 When Perception Fails

Examine Figure 2.3. Here, the senses process a series of parallel oblique lines which, because of the alternating hash marks, appear not to be parallel at all. If you could back up a sufficient distance from the diagram you would see, as the distracting hash marks fade into the oblique lines, that the lines are in fact parallel. The brain has misinterpreted some of the visual information. We refer to this type of visual error as an *optical illusion*. Such illusions dramatically demonstrate the difference between sensation and perception in our visual world.

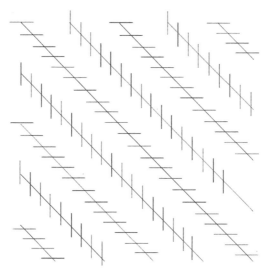

Figure 2.3 *In this illusion, called the* Herrringbone Illusion, *the parallel oblique lines are perceived to slant away from one another because of the conflicting visual information provided by the horizontal and vertical hash marks.*

Illusions can be found in everyday situations. For example, people commonly underestimate the length of dashed lane markings as shorter than they actually are (Harte, 1975). Most people estimate that the markings are between 0.6 to 1.5 m (2 to 5 feet) when in fact they are normally between 3 to 5.5 m (10 to 18 feet) in length.

Illusions point out in a dramatic way that objects in the visual field are not viewed in isolation. Rather, the brain clearly interprets relationships between these objects, and these relationships form our perception of any particular situation. Even though the oblique lines in the Herringbone Illusion are parallel, their relationship to the hash marks can not be ignored by the brain; the final perception is one which is entirely different from the image that would have emerged if the hash marks had not been present. Psychologists refer to this phenomenon as *gestalt* from the German word meaning "whole" or "pattern."

The critical element is the fact that our actions are guided by our perceptions. Our perception of the entire visual field may be quite different from our perception of the individual elements within that visual field. A good example of this is the moon illusion. When the moon is viewed just above the horizon, especially during times of a full moon, it appears huge, yet as it rises well above the horizon it appears much smaller in size. If you were to view the moon just above the horizon in isolation, through a rolled-up paper tube for example, the moon would appear to shrink down to its expected size. One explanation for this illusion is that when the moon is just above the horizon we judge its size based on its relation to other objects such as buildings and trees. When the moon is high in the sky, these other objects no longer serve as visual cues, and so the moon does not appear to be as large. Looking through the paper tube also has the effect of eliminating the visual cues and so the moon appears smaller when viewed in this way.

Perception is not possible without sensation, but perception is much more than sensation. It is an interpretation of sensation based on individual experience and based on the relationships between all of the elements present at the time the sensation is experienced. Adding, subtracting, or modifying any of the sensory elements may entirely change the resulting perception. If we were to remove the horizontal and vertical hash marks from Figure 2.3, for example, the oblique lines would suddenly appear to be parallel. Complex judgements, such as those required in the perception of distance and speed frequently involve the simultaneous interpretation of many sensory elements and create conditions that are ripe for misperception.

2.12 Perception of Distance and Speed

Judgements involving distance and speed of objects in our visual fields are very, very complex. We rely on a variety of cues, some physiological and some external, to make these difficult judgements.

We are essentially stereoscopic viewers of the world around us. That is to say, we can perceive depth and judge distance partly because we have two eyes placed in the front of the head, each of which receives slightly different visual images. You can demonstrate this by holding a finger out in front of you and alternately closing first just your left eye and then just the right eye while focusing on the background. The image of your finger will appear to jump back and forth against the background, a phenomenon referred to as *retinal disparity*. The brain receives both images and superimposes them into one visual image that contains a powerful perception of depth that is not shared by creatures that have eyes placed at the sides of their heads. In addition to processing the retinal disparity, the brain processes the muscular strain associated with having to turn the eyes inward to focus on an object that is getting closer to the eyes. This process is called *convergence*. As an object gets closer, the amount of inward turn of the eyes necessary to keep the object focused increases, thus increasing the muscular strain. These processes allow us to judge an object's distance, relative to the background from what are referred to as *binocular cues*, or those that are associated with having two eyes and two slightly different visual fields. Binocular cues are only useful in judging distances for objects that are less than about 100 meters away (324 feet), about the length of a football field.

Several additional cues, called monocular cues, are not dependent on having two eyes, nor are they limited to relatively short distances:

- Linear perspective: As parallel lines such as railroad tracks, the edges of a roadway, sidewalks and the like recede into the distance, they appear to converge or come together at the horizon.
- Aerial perspective: Objects that are far away look fuzzy or blurred while near objects look clear.
- Texture: Near objects appear to have rougher or more detailed textures compared to the fine textures or seeming lack of texture of objects that are farther away.
- Interposition: Objects that obscure or partially cover up other objects are judged by us to be nearer.
- Relative sizes: Objects that are farther away look smaller than closer objects that we know to be about the same actual size.
- Light and shadow: As objects get closer, they appear to get brighter, whereas objects that get farther away appear to get dimmer.
- Accommodation: When the eye is focused on an object the degree of bulging of the lens (near objects) or flattening of the lens (distant objects) provides a cue about the distance of the object.
- Motion parallax: Images of moving objects at different distances from the eye travel at different speeds across the retina providing cues about relative distances. Near objects provide fast moving retinal images while distant objects provide slow moving retinal images.

Taken together, the combination of binocular and monocular cues provide us with a powerful and diverse set of strategies for judging an object's distance.

Judging speed for moving objects depends on the ability to sense motion around us. Clearly, any object whose image appears to be moving across the retina will be judged as moving, and the greater the displacement of the image over a given time period, the greater will be the judged speed. We know, however, that the size of the object can affect perception of speed, with larger objects being perceived to move more slowly than small objects. Additionally, eye movements that occur while tracking a moving object would also provide motion information for the brain, with faster eye movements being associated with faster moving objects. Tracking an object, however, slows the movement of the object's image across the retina, producing a perception of slower speed when compared to keeping the eyes and head still. The combined slowing effects of *tracking* a *large* moving object, such as a train, may explain why people frequently misjudge the speed of trains as slower than they actually are, and thereby collide with them. Conversely, of course, one would expect people to overestimate the speed of visually small objects such as motorcycles, bicycles and the like, however, this effect might be counterbalanced to some extent by a *tracking-produced* slowing perception.

Judging distance and speed are extremely complex abilities that require a tremendous amount of information processing. This may, occasionally, produce conflicting messages to the brain which result in misperception. Safely operating a motor vehicle requires judgements of both speed and distance for other objects, which is made even more difficult when the perceiver is in motion. Each collision must be examined with respect to the required judgements of the involved operators. An understanding of the basic processes can only serve as a guide to help one consider what judgements each operator may have faced. The opportunity for error is high when drivers in motion are required to judge the relative distances and speeds of other objects in motion.

Examine Figure 2.4a. In this illusion, two lines of equal lengths are perceived by us to be of different lengths. The illusion is produced by the location and orientation of the lines. If we change the location of the vertical line, sliding it to the right for example, to form a right angle as seen in Figure 2.4b, the illusion disappears. One of the most important cues allowing us to judge distance between us and an object is the apparent size of the object. The orientation and location of the object with respect to other objects in the visual field may affect our perception of its distance. Further, we use apparent changes in size of an object to judge its speed of motion. Thus our judgements of both distance and speed of other objects is not independent of where those objects are placed in the visual field. Whether such illusions translate into actual errors made by drivers and observers is not known, but it is obvious that the potential exists and must be respected.

In spite of the many converging cues available to humans to judge the separation distances and speeds of other objects, we perform poorly at such tasks. This is evidenced by the frequency of collisions in which drivers turn their vehicles into the paths of other motorists or attempt to cross roadways in front of them. In general terms drivers are just not very good at judging arrival times of other vehicles (the times that it will take for other vehicles to reach them), nor are they very good at judging the speeds of other vehicles, especially unusually large or unusually small vehicles such as trains and motorcycles. This will be particularly true for narrow approach angles (close to head-on approaches). Olson (2003) suggests that while there exists a public belief that drivers make such judgements as closing speed of other vehicles with some accuracy, the available literature reveals that they do it very poorly.

Generally, decisions that drivers make about whether it is safe to enter a roadway, to turn left in front of a vehicle approaching from the left, for example, are based on the proximity of the approaching vehicles. Drivers make assumptions about arrival times of conflicting vehicles based on their past experience with vehicles at similar distances. They make judgements about whether or not they will have sufficient time to complete the entry maneuver based on location. Unfortunately, that past experience is very likely based on approach speeds at or about the speed limit. When approaching vehicles are traveling very quickly this decision-making strategy frequently leads to collisions.

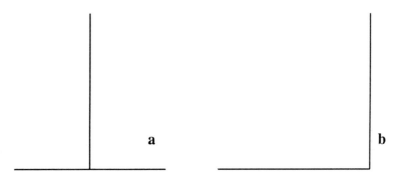

Figure 2.4 *In this line illusion, (a) the vertical line appears to be longer than the horizontal line. If you measure them, you will find that they are the same length. Could such illusions lead to some potential errors in judging distances and speeds of vehicles? Notice that if the vertical line is moved to the right so that it no longer bisects the horizontal line, (b) the illusion disappears.*

2.13 Processing Speed and Time

As indicated at the beginning of this chapter, motor vehicle collisions are ephemeral events lasting only small parts of a second in time. Within that time period, many individual events have occurred: The vehicles or objects have collided and begun to separate, the occupants have moved with respect to the vehicles and perhaps collided with the vehicle interiors or with each other, and air bags, if present and activated, have deployed and begun to deflate. What events, if any, could a normal person reasonably observe in such a short period of time? The human brain and nervous system are often likened to a computer, but while the transmission of information in computers is electrical in nature and consequently moves very fast (about 300,000 km/sec or 186,000 miles per second), the medium of transmission in the human nervous system relies on chemical interactions. By comparison to a computer, information in the nervous system moves at a snail's pace, typically about .10 km/sec or .062 miles per second (Carlson, 1990).

This slow processing speed limits how quickly events can be fed into the human senses before they can no longer be distinguished from one another. Motion pictures and video images take advantage of this limitation by presenting visual images at a rate (about 30 images per second for video) that exceeds the human capacity for processing separate images. The result is that an enormous collection of still images presented sequentially appears to be continuous, seamless, realistic motion.

Some readers may remember the concept of subliminal advertising made popular in the 1960s and 1970s. The idea was that it might be possible to unconsciously perceive something presented too quickly for conscious perception. As an example, hidden advertising messages such as "Drink Coke!" flashed intermittently between the actual film frames of a movie shown in theaters. The intention was to get theater patrons to order Coke at the refreshment stand without a conscious awareness that their buying behavior was being influenced by the "hidden" messages. Empirical research has shown little or no support for this idea. "Subliminal" means literally below the threshold of human perception and it would appear from the available evidence that information presented at a subliminal level has no significant effect on human behavior. Many events surrounding collisions, like the hidden advertising messages, are much too brief to be processed consciously. We must not expect that such events will be processed at some *subliminal* or *subconscious* level.

The slowness of information transfer in our nervous systems accounts for perception-reaction times which, when compared to machines, are fairly long. Olson (1996), after reviewing a substantial body of literature on driver perception and response, concluded that a reasonable perception-reaction time for most drivers in the most straightforward driving situations would fall between 0.75 and 1.5 seconds after the first appearance of an unexpected object of interest into the driver's field of view. An anticipated encounter would reasonably require less time. That range of values might vary slightly depending on a number of situational factors. What value should we assign the eyewitness for perception and response? Should it be the same as for drivers? This is not an area that has, to my knowledge, received specific scientific attention. When considering perception-reaction times for the driver we normally consider that the total duration encompasses a number of steps (Olson, 1989):

A. Detection: from the time the object of interest first enters the driver's field of view to the time that it rises to conscious awareness

B. Identification: the time that it takes the driver to determine that the object poses a hazard and action will be required

C. Decision: the time that it takes the driver to decide on a course of action

D. Reaction: the time that it takes the driver to initiate the desired action, usually braking or steering

To the extent that an observer's task involves the eyewitness equivalent of all four of these stages, we might reasonably assume a similar range of values for eyewitness' perception-reaction times. In many situations, however, the eyewitness need only engage in the first and last of these stages. If we think about an eyewitness who says that his attention was drawn to the sound of screeching tires or to the sound of the crash itself, causing him to turn around and look, then the detection of the event is followed almost immediately by the response. In such circumstances we could reasonably conclude that the duration of his perception-response time might be considerably shorter for such an eyewitness than for a driver involved in the same event.

2.14 Perception of Time

Eyewitnesses consistently overestimate the time duration of events. Loftus (1996) tells us that "people almost invariably overestimate the amount of time something took. When the event is over and they are thinking back and trying to provide an accurate estimate of how long it took, classically, they estimate a duration that is too long" (p. 227). The degree of overestimation is not trivial. In a study by Loftus, Schooler, Boones and Kline (1987), subjects who viewed a thirty second event gave an average estimate for the duration of the event of 150 seconds, a fivefold increase. Ainsworth (1998) describes another danger of this overestimation:

> Earlier we mentioned that people seem to believe that the longer witnesses have to view a scene, the more likely they are to be accurate in their memory. If witnesses overestimate the length of time they had to view a scene by a factor of up to five, then a false impression may be created in the minds of jurors evaluating such testimony. (pp. 36–37)

Of course, we can not generalize this degree of overestimation from one experiment to real life; the dramatic fivefold overestimation might have been unique to that particular study's context. Nonetheless, the phenomenon exists and its importance in eyewitness testimony should not be discounted.

This phenomenon of time overestimation by witnesses may be related to a similar curiosity in which drivers, occupants, and witnesses frequently report a feeling of time elongation during a traumatic event. People frequently report that time seemed to stand still or everything happened in slow motion. I suspect that both time overestimation and time elongation phenomena are related to a change in physiological state. Collisions, even minor ones, are traumatic events for the people involved. It is not hard to imagine that under such conditions, people experience a sudden rise in their adrenaline levels. Adrenaline, properly called epinephrine, is the body's natural stimulant, and increased levels would promote, among other effects, pupil dilation and faster information processing in the nervous system, allowing people to process more information per unit of time than before the epinephrine increase. Our subjective experience of time, the way that we define and understand it, is inextricably tied to an observed series of events in the world around us. This idea is best grasped by listening to young children who relate the passage of time, quite literally, to events. A child might for example describe a period of days as so many sleeps, or the concept of tomorrow as one more sleep. If the nervous system is suddenly processing more information per actual unit of time (during the rise in epinephrine levels) and our perception of time is based on the number of events that are occurring, then the subjective impression will be that time is slowing down relative to our normal experience. In other words, if we gauge how fast time is passing by how much we perceive every second, and that amount increases, then our perception will be a corresponding increase in time.

My explanation for the time distortion phenomena is clearly speculative, but it appears to be consistent with Loftus' (1996) report which found, "Filled intervals are perceived to be longer. So it may be that it has something to do with the fact that many things are happening in the interval and, in a stressful interval, relatively, even more things are happening within the interval" (p. 228). The underlying cognitive processes that produce the subjective time misperceptions of witnesses and participants in their anecdotal reports still await scientific enquiry. But while we may not fully understand the underlying processes that lead to time distortions, we must no less be concerned about their effects. The evidence is clear that they exist whether we understand them or not.

2.15 Perception and Knowledge

While investigating an intersection collision, I once interviewed a young woman who claimed that she had seen "the whole thing". She told me that one vehicle was southbound and was struck on the right rear wheel well by an eastbound vehicle, causing the southbound vehicle to rotate counterclockwise and travel to final rest on the east side of the intersection. The damage to the vehicles was entirely consistent with her telling, but the direction of rotation was not consistent with physical laws. An examination of the physical evidence at the scene revealed that the southbound vehicle was in fact northbound and was struck on the right rear by a westbound vehicle. She clearly had not seen it "all". She very likely saw the final rest positions of the vehicles, and from that information drew an inference about how the vehicles arrived there. But why did she get the rotation wrong? Later, I asked her to show me, with her hands representing the vehicles, how the two cars came together and separated. She made the same error. It became clear to me that she had no understanding of vehicle dynamics, and therefore the dynamic that she suggested made as much sense to her as anything else.

This example reminds me that people will base their perception of events on past experience and knowledge. If that knowledge base contains errors then so may the resulting perceptions. Most collision witnesses see some of the events, but miss many more, leaving gaps or holes in their mental pictures of the events. I have a friend who worked as a collision reconstructionist for a large metropolitan police force. He told me that he routinely asked the following question when interviewing witnesses: "Can you tell me what drew your attention to the collision?" If the answer were akin to "I heard the crash and turned around," then he knew that they could not have observed the collisions themselves. At best, they might have seen the vehicles at or approaching their final rest positions.

The human mind prefers closure and completeness in order for us to properly organize and interpret, for memory, the events that we have observed. Thus, it is inevitable that we will fill in the missing pieces based on our understanding of the world around us. In other words, based on our experience and knowledge, we attempt to reconstruct the series of events that we just observed because, as we will learn in the next chapter, material which is disjointed, disorganized, and incomplete with respect to meaning is very difficult to remember.

2.16 Perception and Expectation

You no doubt have heard the expression, "We see what we want to see and we hear what we want to hear." Perhaps a better way of expressing this sentiment would be to say that the way in which we perceive events around us is affected by our expectations for those events. Psychologists refer to our sets of expectations as *mental sets*. In a study designed to explore this concept, Bugelski and Alampay (1961) had subjects view a number of figures. One group viewed a series of drawings depicting human faces while another group viewed a series of animal drawings. Both groups were then presented with a final ambiguous drawing which could be seen as either a bald man in profile wearing glasses or as a rat. Subjects' perceptions of the final figure as a man or as a rat depended almost entirely on which group of figures they had seen first.

That the effects of expectation are not limited to visual perception can be demonstrated in the following way: Ask a friend to pronounce aloud the words that you will write on a piece of paper, and write the following words, allowing him or her to pronounce each one as you finish writing it: croak, poke, soak, and folk. Now ask your friend the following question: What do you call the white of an egg? Your friend will almost surely say yolk. This little trick is based on establishing a pattern of responding in the subject so that he or she comes to expect that the answer to the question will be related to the common sounds of the previous items.

Loftus and Palmer (1974) showed subjects a film depicting an automobile accident and then asked them to estimate how fast the vehicles were going. The actual question varied the descriptive word for the impact. Some subjects were asked: About how fast were the cars going when they hit each other? Other subjects received the same question except that the word "hit" was replaced by "smashed," "collided," "bumped," or "contacted." The speed estimates given by the subjects varied according to the descriptor used. "Smashed" resulted in the highest speed estimate of 40.8 mph and "contacted" resulted in the lowest speed estimate of 30.8 mph. All subjects viewed the same film, and yet different subjects developed different perceptions of the vehicles' motions depending on the leading descriptors.

2.17 Perception and Truth

Some years ago I came across a cartoon in which an elderly man and his grandson stood in a snow drift in their yard. The grandfather says, "This is nothing! Why when I was your age the snow came right up to my chin." The snow was at thigh level for the grandfather and certainly far removed from the mammoth drifts of snow from his childhood memories. The humor of the cartoon is found by looking at the child standing beside his grandfather with…you guessed it…snow right up to his chin. The cartoon teaches us an important lesson about the nature of human perception, which is that it is entirely dependent on past experience. Both people, the old man and the child, are observing the same event—one from an adult point of view with a lifetime of experience with such events and the other, as a child and brand new viewer. While both received the same sensory input, their perceptions and importantly their future memories of this event, will be dramatically different.

This leads us to an inescapable conclusion regarding human perception of collisions: There are no absolute truths in eyewitness observations of motor vehicle collisions, there are only perceptions of truth. Each observer interprets the events of the collision in light of their personal significance. Peoples' perceptions of the events are a product of many factors, including, but not limited to their knowledge and abilities, expectations, emotional involvement and levels of stress, background, environment, attitudes, motives, and beliefs.

Loftus (1996) describes witnessing a traffic collision as consisting of three stages: acquisition, retention, and retrieval. In this chapter I have described some of the limitations of human sensation and perception, essentially what Loftus has described as the acquisition stage. In the next two chapters I will discuss human memory and forgetting which, taken together, will encompass retention and retrieval.

Chapter 3

Human Memory:
I Have a Pretty Good Memory;
It's Just a Little Short

Memory is what defines each of us as an individual. It is what Fischbach and Coyle (1995) have called "the scaffolding upon which all mental life is constructed." Without memory we could not be aware, could neither speak nor listen, could not plan, dream, wish or imagine. We could do none of the things that we call "human," things that distinguish us from all the other creatures that inhabit this world. We would simply live in the present, repetitively and reflexively responding to the world with no knowledge of the past and no vision of the future.

As a child I used to spend hours wadding up small bits of paper and pitching them into spider webs, observing that each and every time a wad was trapped by a web, its owner would rush out from the hub of the web. In preparing to spin its sticky manacles around the paper victim to prevent its escape, it would discover the ruse, release the wad, and with what seemed to me to be disdain, cast it out of the web where it fell unceremoniously to the ground. The spiders would then make the necessary repairs to their webs and return home empty-handed. The spiders never seemed to tire of this game. Each and every time I pitched a decoy into the webs, they would fruitlessly attack. While I came to admire the relentless perseverance of the creatures, I more importantly came to appreciate the enormous benefits of memory, and the resultant ability to learn from experience.

The major task of an eyewitness is to accurately recall a set of observations or actions that occurred at an earlier point in time. Clearly, such a task is entirely dependent on memory. In this chapter, we will explore the nature of human memory and then focus on its limitations with respect to the all important task that each observer of a collision will face: recalling that which he or she had observed or done.

3.1 The Nature of Memory

Memory is more than just a random collection of experiences in the brain. It is an organized collection of experiences that enable us to make behavioral decisions. This must be so. Imagine that you have randomly placed every piece of paper that you've ever read into an enormous filing cabinet. With the addition of each new piece, the search time to locate any particular piece would be extended. Your decision making, if it relied on finding one or other of the stored documents, would become longer and longer until eventually, you would be unable to find a particular document and so be unable to make decisions.

Imagine further that one day you are walking along, minding your own business, when you unexpectedly come across another creature. You open your mental filing cabinet searching frantically through the random collection for any piece of paper that concerns animals. You then scan each one, searching for the one that correctly describes the creature standing in front of you. When you find the right piece you have to read it carefully to discover whether or not you should run. Had the creature been a large and hungry carnivorous animal, your search time would likely have exceeded your lifetime. This decision-making function of memory is succinctly described by Squire (1995), as he states, "our species seems best adapted for accumulating knowledge—for inference, approximation, concept formation, and classification—not for the literal retention of the individual exemplars that lead to and support general knowledge" (p. 220). To be useful, a memory system must be organized. Humans must make frequent and rapid decisions, so any sensible memory system must facilitate quick and easy access to stored information. But human memory, no matter how well organized, can not handle limitless amounts of information. Therefore, effective memory must also be selective. An ideal memory then, for human beings, would be both well organized and selective. It would also be flexible, capable of holding on to information for as long as it might be required, yet equally capable of quickly discarding useless information. Most often we only need to hold on to information for brief periods of time, such as a telephone number that we'll only use once, and occasionally we need to retain a piece of information for a lifetime, like our names. Human memory is capable of processing events at different levels of permanency. We can conveniently refer to these levels as sensory memory, short-term memory (STM), and long-term memory (LTM). Each level of processing satisfies a unique set of needs that, together, allow us to function effectively as human beings.

3.2 Sensory Memory

The world bombards our senses with stimuli. Sights, sounds, smells, tastes and tactile feelings fall upon us like rain. If we were to try to process everything and store everything that we processed, we would quickly become drenched, unable to absorb anything more without losing the information as overflow. At the outset then, our memory system must be capable of choosing what stimuli to process. This is accomplished through selective attention. Attention can be deliberate, as when we choose to examine the details of an automobile in the showroom, or automatic, as when the sound of screeching tires or crushing metal draws our attention to a crash. If standing in front of me is a growling beast with its enormous canine teeth dripping saliva, I don't need to count the number of toes it has or note the shade of its fur to appreciate that now would be a good time to retreat. Similarly, a motorcyclist cresting a hill and encountering an overturned tractor-trailer obstructing the roadway need not observe the number of axles on the trailer or the color of the tractor to decide that braking hard would be sensible. When a sufficient number of details about an event have been processed, one can decide on a course of action. The remaining details are superfluous and extremely unlikely to be processed at all. Attention is an initial perceptual process, as is the first type of memory that we will discuss: sensory memory.

Sensory memory refers to the ability to retain sensory images long enough to decide whether they warrant additional processing. If you stare at this page for a few moments and then close your eyes, you can still see the page for about one-half second or so. This is the temporal duration of sensory memory for visual information. After one-half second the visual image will have faded away. Sensory memory for sounds is slightly longer, having a duration of about three to four seconds, after which the sound will have faded away. To keep sights and sounds in your mind longer than a few seconds you will either have to look at the object or hear the sound again, or process the information at a deeper level while it is still in the sensory memory.

Research into visual sensory memory (Sperling, 1960) suggests that virtually everything within the visual field is accessible for that brief half-sec-

ond. Sperling showed subjects numbers and letters arranged in rows of varying lengths for very brief periods of time and then asked subjects to recall as
many digits as they could. The results suggested that most subjects could recall
only about four, suggesting that the capacity of the sensory memory is severely
limited. Then Sperling presented subjects with the combinations again but
this time, just as the stimuli were removed from sight, he cued subjects about
which row he wanted them to recall by presenting an auditory signal. Some
subjects were required to recall the top row, some the bottom row, and others,
the middle row. Subjects, regardless of which row was requested, performed
equally well. This result suggested that the subjects took in the entire visual image, but by the time they recalled and wrote about four characters, the image
had faded. This type of research indicates that people have available, for a brief
period of time, all the information in the focused visual field. The specific images in that visual field, however, quickly disappear and are lost forever unless
they are acted on immediately and processed at a deeper level. Thus sensory
memory appears to have an enormous capacity but its duration is fleeting.

3.3 Short-Term Memory

In order to remember information for longer than a few seconds, we must
quickly decide to process it in a more permanent fashion. The next stage of
permanency in the memory process is short-term memory (STM), which is
sometimes referred to as working memory and is akin to RAM or random
access memory in a computer. STM is a process in which the information of
interest, such as an initial series of events from a traffic crash, is temporarily
retained with the intent of trying to understand its meaning or importance
for future action. Unlike sensory memory, STM is accompanied by a specific
conscious awareness of the sensation of interest. It is at this stage that we
become subjectively aware of the event. While we rarely articulate what is
happening in STM it might be something like, "What just happened? What
did I just see or hear? Do I need to remember this event? Will it affect me
in some way? Do I have some preexisting knowledge that will help me to
understand this event?" In other words, it is at this stage that we begin to
decide the significance of and need to remember a new event.

Earlier, I discussed the need for organization in memory, to ensure that
if we need to recall an event, it can be found quickly. STM represents a pre-
liminary organizational process in which a first attempt is made to connect a
new stimulus event to an existing knowledge base to make the new memory
available for retrieval.

Just as a computer's working memory or RAM has capacity limitations,
so too does human STM. Traditionally, the capacity of STM is measured by

presenting individuals with a series of items on a number of successive trials and then having them recite the series back again, increasing the length of the series with each trial. Eventually a point is reached where subjects begin to consistently make errors in reciting the list of items. This point would represent the limit or capacity of short-term memory. In this fashion, the capacity of STM was discovered to be limited to about seven *chunks* of information (Miller, 1956). It may be more than mere coincidence that telephone numbers used to be seven digits in length. But if the limit of short-term memory is about seven chunks, how then is it possible for us to remember a series of things that is longer than this, a feat which we frequently accomplish? The secret lies in understanding the special meaning of the word chunk. A chunk is the smallest meaningful unit of information to be retained. If I were to give you a series of random numbers to remember, you would probably begin to make errors when the series exceeded about seven numbers. But what if the series looked like this: 2, 4, 6, 8, 10, 12, 14, 16, 18, 20, and so forth? You could probably retain a never ending string of such numbers because, to reproduce the set you would need only three chunks of information: the first number in the series, the last number in the series, and the rule that they are successive even integers. We have managed to reduce what initially appeared to be ten items of information to only three simply by understanding the relationship between the items. In a similar fashion, as people learn language they learn to chunk letters into words, words into sentences, and sentences into entire passages, eventually enabling them to reduce enormous amounts of information into manageable bits that can be successfully retained. The limits of STM, then, are really dependent on the individual's ability to find meaningful relationships between the pieces of information. At this task individuals vary widely in their abilities. Information which can not be meaningfully related is still limited to about seven items.

Despite the powerful increases in information capacity that can be accomplished by chunking, STM is still limited. Some effective filtering or selection system must operate to prevent information overload. Short-term memory operates in multiple sensory channels so that we can see and hear at the same time, for example, or walk and talk simultaneously. But overload can occur within a particular sensory channel. To demonstrate this I often have students try to write down an unfamiliar word which I say out loud for them, antidisestablishmentarianismist, for example, and while writing it they must sing a familiar song. Because writing down an unfamiliar word requires that they mentally hear the word in order to reproduce it, and because singing also requires them to mentally hear the song in order to sing it, the result is that the two tasks interfere with one another and they are unable to do both. Generally they switch back and forth between the tasks, writing a little, then singing a little, then writing a little more, but when they are writing they are not singing and when they are singing they are not writing. So, while an effective selection process is important at the sensory memory level, at the level of short-term memory it is imperative.

It was purportedly Confucious, the Chinese philosopher, who said, "A picture is worth a thousand words." Right now I would bet that you could close your eyes and picture yourself standing in front of your home and describe in great detail a reasonably accurate description of what you see in your mind's eye. Visual images are perhaps the ultimate demonstrations of information chunking. When you imagine a visual image, an enormous number of items of information are brought to bear in working memory in an instant. That we can perform this amazing achievement suggests that our memories are most effective when we are processing visual information.

As a demonstration of the effectiveness of human memory for visual information, I always have participants in my human factors lectures engage in the following exercise.[1] First I distribute a set of typed instructions. For half the participants, the instructions read as follows: "Please rate the sentences I will read aloud on how easily you can pronounce them. Repeat the sentences silently to yourself." This set of instructions is designed to get the participants to process the information in an auditory fashion. The other half of the participants receive a different set of instructions: "Please rate the sentences I will read aloud on how well you can form a vivid mental picture or image of the action of the sentence." This set of instructions is intended to get the participants to process the information in a visual fashion. To both groups I then read aloud twenty sentences such as: "The chocolate choo-choo train chugged down the licorice tracks," and "The silly snake slithered down a steep sliding board." After presenting all twenty sentences I then quiz the participants, asking twenty questions about what they have just heard, such as: Who slithered down a steep sliding board? and What chugged down the licorice tracks? and so on. The participants then score themselves out of a maximum score of twenty points, one for each correct answer. The differences in the scores between the two groups is astounding, with the visual instructions group averaging fifteen or more correct answers and the auditory instructions group averaging a mere seven or eight correct responses (just about what one would expect if the auditory group were relying on short-term memory alone).

This exercise has never failed in the many years that I have been using it, but what does it tell us about short-term memory? First, the results of the

---

1   This exercise is attributed to Don Irwin and Janet Simons from the Developmental Educational Learning Institute in Des Moines, IA, 1993.

above exercise suggest that some kinds of information, such as visual information, are more accurately and reliably processed than others, like auditory information. If the information is more effectively processed, it is more effectively remembered. Thus we might place more stock in witness's recollections of what they saw than in what they heard. It also becomes apparent that the specific methods that we choose to process information can determine how well we are likely to process and remember that information. It might be possible, therefore, to train people to more effectively process and remember information by deliberately instructing them to visualize events during the STM stage. If different individuals possess a natural tendency to process the same information in different ways, then some individuals may be more accurate and reliable witnesses than others. If we could ascertain an individual's natural predisposition as a visualizer or as a listener, we might have a useful discriminatory tool for identifying the most promising witnesses.

Are there known limits as to how long information can remain in short-term memory before it disappears? The answer is both yes and no. To find out the duration of STM, early attempts by psychologists involved presenting individuals with items of information followed by predetermined time delays, such as thirty seconds or one minute. After the specified delay the individuals would be asked to recall the items. These first attempts suggested that people could remember bits of information for very long periods of time, but it was soon discovered that the method was flawed: during the delay period the subjects were *rehearsing* or mentally repeating the to-be-remembered information. To prevent rehearsal researchers invented interfering tasks for subjects to engage in during the delay period. For example, after hearing a list of items, subjects might be asked to count aloud backwards by three's from some starting number until the end of the delay period. Armed with these methodological improvements, researchers soon discovered that information can be retained in STM, without rehearsal, for about twenty to thirty seconds, after which the information fades away. Of course, information can be voluntarily discarded sooner than that if it is no longer needed. Have you ever looked up a telephone number in the phone book, retained it long enough to dial it and then mentally discarded it once the phone began to ring through? No doubt you regretted that decision when the call, assuming you are old enough to have lived In the times of live telephone operators, was answered by the operator asking you which number you were calling. At this point you scrambled for the phone book and looked up the number once more, vowing never to voluntarily discard such information again.

Information in short-term memory is short-lived, twenty to thirty seconds, or even less if voluntarily discarded. Alternatively, it can be retained almost indefinitely with rehearsal. Have you ever crammed for an exam the night before? If you have, then you probably remember retaining the information long enough to get through the exam, but as soon as you handed in your paper the information disappeared. This is a very common example of information held in STM by rehearsal. Occasionally, we notice that if we rehearse a piece of information often enough some of it stays with us for a long period of time. This suggests that without necessarily intending to, we have processed that item in a more permanent fashion. The final level of permanency, representing the deepest level of information processing, is referred to as long-term memory.

3.4 Long-Term Memory

When we need to retain information for a lifetime, then it must be processed very differently from what we have discussed so far. Our brief examination of short-term memory revealed that it is severely limited in both its duration (twenty to thirty seconds without rehearsal) and its capacity (about seven chunks). As far as we can discern, long-term memory (LTM) has no practical limits regarding duration or capacity. As we have discussed, filtering systems exist at the level of sensory and short-term memory to prevent us from overtaxing our storage capacities. Since this filter operates before the information reaches long-term memory, the extent to which we actually test our long-term memory capacities is limited. Nonetheless, I have yet to hear a complaint from anyone stating they ran out of long-term memory space. While nothing lasts forever, it is evident that information stored as long-term memory will last a lifetime, which for most of us, is undoubtedly long enough.

Recent studies of memory at a biological level suggest that the transition from short-term to long-term memory may be associated with molecular changes at a neural level during the consolidation phase (Abel et al., 1995). This is a period of time in which chemical changes take place in the brain that produce permanent memory traces or connected patterns of neural activity:

> Short-term memory lasts from minutes to hours, whereas long-term memory lasts days, weeks, or even years. The switch from short- to long-term memory is characterized by a consolidation period, during which memory is changed from a labile form that is sensitive to disruption to a stable, self maintained form. (Abel et al., 1995, p. 298)

According to this view, long-term memory does not occur immediately. Rather, some delay exists in which presumably, the necessary chemical changes in the brain transpire. It follows that during this delay, the information which is intended for permanent storage is ripe for distortion and influence.

At a subjective level, the transition of information from temporary to permanent storage involves mental activity. Whereas the maintenance of information in STM primarily involves mental repetition, the transfer to LTM predominately involves associating the new information with existing memory. Somehow we must connect that which is newly acquired to that which we already know. This can't be the only mechanism of transfer. If it were, then how would the first bits of information ever have been permanently stored?

Some mechanism exists that allows repetitively processed information to be stored as well. This fits with our experience that information that we have rehearsed often enough attains permanence. Telephone numbers are probably transferred from short- to long-term memory in this fashion. Unfortunately, the transfer of information to LTM by simple rehearsal is a happenstance affair; sometimes the transfer is successful but more often it fails. The most effective transfer is accomplished when it stems not from rote activity, but rather from a deliberate effort to examine the meaning of the new material and its connection to existing knowledge (Craik and Lockhart, 1972).

Generally, information retained in short-term memory is stored as we initially perceived it. Keep in mind that individual perceptions of the same event can vary widely amongst observers. Information transferred to long-term memory, however, is seldom a faithful reproduction of the original observation:

> ...when information is tagged for filing in long-term storage, the meaning of the item is more important than its exact physical form. To store or catalog the information, an analysis is performed to determine how it can be added to the things that are already stored. In this analysis, things can be added, left out, or rearranged. Most often a rearranged memory is just as useful as the original version. We don't always need to remember something exactly, but we do need to know what it means. (Huffman, Vernoy, Williams and Vernoy, 1991, pp. 205–206)

Long-term memory is to the original observation what a movie or book review is to the original movie or book. It is not a faithful reproduction of our observations, but an interpretation of the original information. While it may contain the flavor or essence of the original experience with regard to meaning and substance, it is lacking the detail of the original. This must be distinctly understood. If human memory were to be likened to a security system it would function more like a motion detector than a video camera. It would capture movement in the world around it but not capture a detailed visual image. Expecting an eyewitness to recall minute details of a series of events leading up to a motor vehicle collision is rather like examining a motion detector for details of an intruder's appearance; they just aren't there to begin with.

3.5 Memory Distortion

Memory is a reconstructive process. The capacity and duration limitations of sensory and short-term memory dictate that an eyewitness can not process all the details of a motor vehicle collision. While sensory memory can store a large number of details, it can do so for only a brief moment. By the time some of the information is transferred to short-term memory, much of the original detail is lost. The only way to capture additional elements is to examine the scene again, but motor vehicle collisions are dynamic events. By the time the scene is re-examined, it has changed. The result is that information is acquired in an incomplete fashion. It is rather like reading only one or two words from each sentence of this book and then trying to make sense of the entire text. Occasionally you may glean enough to get the gist of a passage, but if you were quizzed on the specific details you would fail miserably. As was discussed earlier, the key to transferring information from short-term to long-term memory lies in finding meaning and associative value in the to-be-stored information. If an eyewitness is catching only random, momentary glimpses of the collision, then the semantic value or meaningfulness of the glimpses may not be apparent. It would be much like masking the eyes in a photograph of an individual's face and then trying to guess who the individual is. Try it sometime and see how difficult a task this would be.

To prevent the information from being lost entirely, the assortment of pieces will have to be meaningfully connected and integrated into the existing knowledge base. This will require the use of assumptions by the eyewitness about the missing pieces. The successful transfer of observations to long-term memory is normally dependent on being able to organize and understand the information. Thus, if the information is incomplete, the eyewitness will have to reconstruct the missing information based on available information from the scene itself, from information provided by others at the scene, and from inferences drawn from the witness's own understanding of the world and how things happen in that world:

...suppose a person sees an automobile accident. The witness is presumed to interpret the accident by calling upon (1) portions of the initial input, that is, the accident itself; (2) ideas from his store of general knowledge (about accidents, intersections, and pedestrians, for example); and (3) inferences. The inferences are likely aspects of the situation which have not actually been observed; thus upon realizing that an accident occurred, a person might infer that some damage was done either to the car or the pedestrian. Fragments of this interpretation are then stored in memory. (Loftus, 1996, p. 112)

Much of our present understanding of the reconstructive nature of memory comes from an impressive body of work by Elizabeth Loftus and her colleagues in the 1970s. A typical procedure used by these researchers would require subjects to view a film or group of slides portraying a crime or traffic collision. Subjects would then be quizzed on what they had seen. For half the subjects, a bit of misinformation would be embedded in the questionnaire. The other half would receive veridical information. The subjects would then be required to recall the original events (Loftus, 1996). As an example, consider a study by Loftus, Miller, and Burns (1978). Here, all subjects were shown a series of slides portraying a collision of an automobile with a pedestrian.

The critical slide was one in which a car was stopped either at a stop sign for half the subjects, or at a yield sign for the other half. Subjects then filled out a twenty-item questionnaire. For half of the subjects, one of the items read, "Did another car pass the red Datsun while it was stopped at the stop sign?" For the other half, the question asked was, "Did another car pass the red Datsun while it was stopped at the yield sign?" After a short filler activity subjects were then shown a series of slides presented in pairs, one of which they had already seen, the other of which was new. Their task was to select the previously viewed slide from each pair. The critical pair was of course the one that presented both the stop sign and yield sign slides together. Subjects who had not been misled in the questionnaire chose the correct slide 75 percent of the time. In contrast, those subjects who had been deliberately misled, chose the correct slide from each pair only 41 percent of the time.

As a demonstration of the reconstructive nature of memory, I have used a modified version of the Loftus, Miller, and Burns procedure on dozens of occasions with large groups of individuals who have come to hear me speak about human factors in traffic crashes. The modification was suggested to me by Elizabeth Loftus in a personal communication. In my modified procedure, I present the original slides at a rate of about one slide per second with the critical slide always depicting the red Datsun stopped at a yield sign, followed by the twenty item questionnaire in which all participants are misled with the statement that the car was stopped at a stop sign. Almost immediately afterward I show three more slides, two previously unviewed filler slides and the critical slide depicting the car stopped at a stop sign. I ask the participants to indicate for each of the three slides, whether it was one of the originally presented slides or not. Almost invariably, anywhere from one-third to one-half or more of the participants indicate, incorrectly, that they had previously seen the car stopped at a stop sign.

I also ask participants to rate their degrees of certainty in each of their choices on a scale from zero percent to 100 percent. There appear to be no substantial differences in the confidence ratings given by correct versus incorrect choices. Interestingly, the confidence ratings given by participants, even those who have chosen incorrectly, are usually between 80 and 100 percent. I always query participants, especially those who have chosen incorrectly, to get a sense of why they have been successfully misled. Generally, those who choose incorrectly state that they did not initially observe what kind of sign existed; their visual focus was on the car, not the sign. The opposite appears to be true for those who respond correctly; they report specifically and consciously observing the sign itself in the original presentation. We can now begin to assemble, from much of the discussion of this and previous chapters, an explanation of why some subjects are misled in the above study. The original slides are presented for only a brief period of time. Participants' visual focus will be drawn to some part of each slide. For the critical slide, the attention of some will be drawn to the car, others to the sign, and still others to some other aspect of the scene. Some may even see both the car and the sign. Earlier, in the section on vision, we discussed the fact that only a small part of the scene depicted in the slide will actually be in sharp focus, that part whose image falls directly on the fovea. The rest of the scene will be out of focus or fuzzy. If your attention were drawn to the car, the car would be in focus while the rest of the scene, including the sign, would be out of focus. Unless you actually looked directly at the sign you would not be able to capture enough detail to determine what kind of sign it was. Thus some subjects would have seen the sign and some would not have. In other words, some subjects would have a less complete memory than others.

The power of the post-event misinformation is strongest on those who did not visually process the nature of the sign initially. They will be particularly sensitive to that information in the misleading question about the stop sign because it represents an opportunity for them to acquire a piece of information that they did not have after viewing the slides alone. That new information, albeit wrong information, is nonetheless stored as a memory for the original event. This is the whole nature of reconstructive memory that Loftus and her colleagues made evident. Once you have stored the information as an original memory, then you ought to be as confident about it as about any other memory. This would explain why no difference is observed in the confidence ratings between those who are misled and those who are not. We will discuss the issue of confidence in some detail later in this chapter.

The misinformation given to subjects in the Loftus, Miller, and Burns study is referred to as misleading post-event information. In a variety of experimental contexts, Loftus and others discovered that subjects presented with inaccurate post-event information have mis-recalled such things as broken glass at the scene of a collision when there was none (Loftus and Palmer, 1974), the color of a car that was green as being blue (Loftus, 1977), a yield sign as a stop sign (already discussed above), tape recorders that never existed (Loftus, 1996), and even something as large and conspicuous as a barn when no barn was ever seen (Loftus, 1975):

> Post-event experiences such as exposure to newly released information can dramatically affect our memory of the original event. Post-event information can not only enhance existing memories but also change a witness's memory and even cause nonexistent details to become incorporated into a previously acquired memory. (Loftus, 1996, p. 54–55)

Taken together, these studies in reconstructive memory suggest that witnesses will take new information, which was never originally experienced, and integrate that information into memory. Subsequently, these modified memories are treated as faithful renditions of the original events.

Not surprisingly, the longer the interval between the original events and the presentation of the post-event misinformation, the greater the influence of the misinformation in affecting subjects' recall (Loftus, Miller, and Burns, 1978). This effect may be related to the loss of information, both correct and incorrect, from memory over the delay, desensitizing the individual to conflicting information which is presented later.

Additionally, the more central or predominant the critical event in the overall scene, the more resistant that original event will be to the effects of misinformation (Loftus, 1996). Thus, while it might have been easy to misdirect subjects about the nature of the stop/yield sign in the Loftus, Miller, and Burns study, a peripheral item in the overall scene, it would likely have been well nigh impossible to misdirect them about the color of the colliding car, a more central feature of the scene.

3.6 Sources of Misinformation in the Real World

In the psychological laboratory post-event misinformation is administered deliberately by the researcher in a carefully planned, controlled fashion so that the effects of false information on a subject's recollections can be observed and identified specifically (much more on this in chapter 5). In the real world, witnesses are exposed to a variety of post-impact sources of information which are for the most part uncontrolled. Witnesses may be questioned by police and other investigators, they may talk with and share information with other participants and witnesses, they may be exposed to a variety of reports of the original events provided by radio, television, and print media. In short, a plethora of information, some consistent and some inconsistent with the original events, is available to the witnesses only a short while after the original events. In time, other sources of information will become available as witnesses may talk to attorneys, read statements provided by others that describe the collision, or read engineering or other technical reports. Up to and sometimes including any court proceedings, witnesses will be exposed to an abundance of information about the collision.

It is not usually obvious to the witness that new information is being provided. Imagine a well-intentioned police officer interviewing a female witness and asking, "Could you estimate the speed of the red car just before the driver slammed on his brakes?" If the witness hadn't previously observed whether the red car was braked or not, she would now have to modify her recollection of the events to include the new information (provided by the officer) that the driver of the red car braked hard. She might infer that there must be skid marks at the scene, and that she should have heard the screeching of tires prior to impact. Remember that inference is an important feature of long-term memory, so the police officer's question would have the effect of increasing the likelihood that the witness would now infer and later recall seeing skid marks and hearing tires screech (Loftus, 1975). Recall the Loftus and Palmer (1974) study cited in the previous chapter, in which subjects were asked to estimate the speed of the vehicles when they "smashed" into or just "hit" one another. One week later subjects were questioned again about the original events and asked specifically, "Did you see any broken glass?" Subjects in the "smashed" condition were much more likely to report broken glass than subjects in the "hit" condition. There was no broken glass in the original series of events. Loftus provides the following caution about post-event information:

Anytime after a witness experiences a complex event, he may be exposed to new information about that event. The new information may come in the form of questions—a powerful way to introduce it —or in the form of a conversation, a newspaper story, and so on. The implications of these results for courtroom examinations, police interrogations, and accident investigations is fairly obvious: interrogators should do whatever possible to avoid the introduction of "external" information into the witness's memory. (Loftus, 1996, p. 78)

As a demonstration of the role of inference and association in creating false memories, I use an adapted version of a classroom demonstration described by Appleby (1986). I read the following list of words to participants: rest, tired, awake, dream, snore, bed, eat, slumber, sound, comfort, wake, and night at a rate of about one every five seconds or so and I ask them to listen carefully and try to remember as many as they can. After presenting the list I ask, by a show of hands: How many of you remember hearing the word aardvark? I haven't yet seen a hand raised to that question. Then I ask: How many of you remember hearing the word sleep? Typically between 50 and 75 percent of the hands go up to this question. Of course, the word sleep was never presented in the first place, yet a large number of people report that it was.

This demonstration has always been a great success, and I think now we can begin to explain why. The original list of words is sufficiently long to ensure that for most participants, short-term memory capacity will have been exceeded and some of the original words will have been lost from short-term memory. The list is also loaded with words that have strong associative value with the target word sleep. (Participants often demonstrate that they are associating the words by pretending to fall asleep or by pretending to snore and the like during the presentation.) Following the initial word list presentation, subjects, not recalling all the words, will fall prey to a combination of expectation and inference. They fill in the missing information based on what they do recall. At the beginning of this chapter I suggested that human memory works best by processing the gist or substance of events that we have experienced, not necessarily the literal representation of those events. The gist of the word list presented to them is sleep, so it is not surprising that a large number of individuals could come to believe that they had heard the word sleep. Based on a number of related words that they still retain in short-term memory, participants may incorrectly infer that sleep must have been one of the original list.

Could similar forces be at work at a collision scene causing witnesses to form false memories of events surrounding the collision? The answer is a resounding yes. Loftus (1996) describes an informal study in which student researchers went to a train station and faked the theft of a tape recorder from a bag, except that no tape recorder was actually removed. The student researchers created the false impression by having a confederate approach an unattended bag and pretend to take something from it. One of the female researchers then returned to her bag and exclaimed, "Oh my God, my tape recorder is missing!" The researchers then began to interact with the eyewitnesses and managed to get their names and telephone numbers. A week later, another student researcher, posing as an insurance agent, called the eyewitnesses and asked about the tape recorder:

> Although there was in fact no tape recorder, over half the witnesses "remembered" seeing it, and nearly all of these could describe it in reasonably good detail. Their descriptions were quite different from one another: some said it was gray and others said black; some said it was in a case and others said it was not; some said it had an antenna, others claimed it did not. Their descriptions indicated a rather vivid "memory" for a tape recorder that was never seen. (Loftus, 1996, p. 62)

Haber and Haber (1999) describe two of the most troubling aspects of post-event information on reports given by witnesses after receiving information from other people. The first is that witnesses will not generally be aware that they have acquired new information and the second is that they will not generally be aware that as a result of the new information, they have actually changed their reports. In the authors' words, "[T]he witnesses remain convinced that they are still reporting an independent memory of what they had originally observed." This conviction on the part of witnesses leads us naturally enough to consider the role that witness confidence plays.

3.7 Witness Overconfidence

Previously, I alluded to the fact that people, even when they are blatantly mistaken, have a high degree of confidence in their recollections of events. As a demonstration of this overconfidence I frequently use a modified adaptation of a procedure used by Milojkovic and Ross (1981). Prior to the commencement of the lecture I take four or five individuals aside and ask that they think of an interesting, brief story to tell the audience. I ask about half of them to tell a true story and the remaining number to tell an entirely fictitious story. I then have each of them tell his or her story. The audience members are asked to guess for each story whether it is the truth or a lie, and to indicate their degree of confidence in their decisions from zero to 100 percent. Each storyteller then reveals whether he told the truth or lied, and audience members score themselves accordingly. Generally, the accuracy of the audience scores are at the chance level or about 50 percent accurate (which would have been achieved if they had merely guessed without having heard the stories first). The interesting result is that the confidence ratings hover around the 70 to 80 percent level. In the original Milojkovic and Ross study, students were found to be 52 percent accurate and 73 percent confident.

The ramifications of an overconfident eyewitness are pretty obvious. First, it is evident that people are likely to be much more confident than they are accurate in judging the veracity of others. This has important implications for triers of fact in judging the credibility of witnesses. Second, it is highly likely that they are much more confident than they are accurate in their recollections of the collision that they observed. Loftus had this to say about eyewitness confidence:

> To reiterate, although there are many studies showing that the more confident a person is in a response, the greater the likelihood that the response is accurate, some studies have shown no relationship at all between confidence and accuracy. In fact, there are even conditions under which the opposite relationship exists between confidence and accuracy, namely, people can be more confident about their wrong answers than their right ones. To be cautious, one should not take high confidence as any absolute guarantee of anything. (Loftus, 1996, p. 101)

Schacter (1995) suggests that one reason that people find memories subjectively compelling is *source amnesia*, in which the content of a past event or imagining becomes 'unglued' from its original source and mistakenly connected to another one. Particularly when a memory contains elements of original observations, once the original source of the event has faded and new information from another source is presented, the elements can exist together and become fused into a new recollection of the original events.

As I write this book I have to be particularly mindful that I paraphrase or quote another author correctly. Additionally, I must be meticulous in citing the original source of any borrowed material so that you, the reader, will be able to identify and locate that source should you wish to read it for yourself. In real life outside this book, however, under normal circumstances, the source of the information that we retain is not nearly as important as the content. Have you ever found yourself saying something like: I read somewhere, though I don't remember the exact source right now, that…? Undoubtedly you have on occasion remembered the content of a magazine article, or a book, or television program, but long since forgotten the source of the information.

If we recall that human memory is a basis for making decisions, then it makes perfect sense that we should be highly confident of our memories. Can you imagine how difficult life would be in the mundane world if we felt that we couldn't trust our own memories? In the movies *Total Recall* and *The Matrix*, the protagonists are cast in dual realities as a result of transplanted artificial memories. Their worlds are emotionally disturbing and confusing as they shuttle back and forth between alternate realities. It is an alienating experience for the main characters as they frequently discover that it is impossible to know exactly who or what to trust. Young children experience a disorientation similar to these characters when they occasionally encounter difficulties distinguishing between their dream states and their wakeful states.

Fortunately, most of us are aware of only one reality in which we learn to trust our recollections and rely on them in our everyday decision making. We build a lifetime of trust in our perceptions and recollections of the world that we encounter. We learn essentially that our memories are, for the most part, accurate. Bear in mind, however, that "accurate" for us means that the essential content or gist of our recollections has been sufficiently well retained to allow us to make decisions regarding our actions. The task of an eyewitness, however, is much greater than this. From an initial interview by police, through the probing of lawyers and finally under the scrutiny of juries and judges, the eyewitness is expected to recall in minute detail a variety of events that may not have been attended to originally, because the witnesses' attention was not drawn to them or if processed, not processed from a forensic point of view. People process events from an autobiographical point of view, not from a physical one:

> This perspective on the functions of autobiographical memory also suggests the reasons people believe that their own memories and those of others are accurate. People are rarely confronted with a contradiction between what they remember happened and the truth, so they have no way to test the accuracy of their memory; most discussions with other people about what is remembered are for the purpose of arriving at a consensus among people, not to check on what actually happened; and finally, most of the changes that occur

in the content of memory occur without awareness so people never realize their memories have altered. (Haber and Haber, 1999)

About fifty years ago, Leon Festinger (1957) published his theory of cognitive dissonance. According to Festinger, when we simultaneously hold two thoughts or cognitions which are in conflict or dissonance, then the result is a state of anxiety or tension. This motivates us to reduce the tension by changing one of the thoughts. The thoughts can be rooted in our attitudes or they can be rooted in our behavior. For example, imagine that in a moment of inattentiveness I have just struck a pedestrian with my vehicle. The thought processes might go something like this: "I have just struck a pedestrian; people who strike pedestrians are careless drivers; I must be a careless driver." Now in conflict with that thought is this idea: "But I am actually a careful driver." We now have a state of cognitive dissonance, which according to Festinger requires resolution and a strong motivation to reduce the dissonance. One option would be for me to change the second cognition from, "I am actually a careful driver," to "I am actually a careless driver, and I will have to change my driving behavior in the future and accept the consequences of this incident." However, an equally effective method of reducing the dissonance would be to change the first cognition to something like: "Pedestrians who are struck by drivers are careless and even the most careful driver is at risk from them, and since I am a careful driver this pedestrian must have acted carelessly." Either way, the dissonance can resolve itself. People, like electricity, usually seek the path of least resistance. Since it is easier to change the first cognition and see the victim as a perpetrator than it is to change our self-images and see ourselves in a bad light, most people elect to change the first cognition rather than the second.

While this is a fascinating area in its own right, it is really only a lead in to an important point about witness overconfidence. Researchers found that people will avoid dissonance by seeking evidence that supports their cognitions and by avoiding information that would contradict them. This ties in directly with the observation of Haber and Haber, in that people are rarely confronted with a contradiction of their memories; it may be explained by the fact that once people have formed their memories of a collision, they are much more inclined to seek supporting rather than contradictory evidence for their memories. Once an eyewitness has formed a recollection of the collision, not only is it highly likely that he or she will seek out confirming information to consolidate those memories, but it is equally likely that he or she will avoid and ignore contradictory information.

3.8 Memory and Emotion

Most people have known for some considerable time now, even if they couldn't explain the reasons why, that emotion and physiology are inextricably bound together. Perhaps you can remember a time when you were angry, and someone offered the advice to take a deep breath and count to ten. The subjective experience of an emotion, such as fear, anger, joy, sadness, disgust, or surprise, is always accompanied by physiological changes in the body, such as increased levels of epinephrine, increased heart rate, increased blood pressure, increased respiration, pupil dilation (enlargement), dry mouth, decreased digestive activity, and increased perspiration. These changes in our bodies ready us for action and have come to be known collectively as the *fight or flight response*, because the changes prepare our bodies to defend us or to flee the threatening situation. Emotion is the subjective or mental counterpart of these physiological changes. In other words, emotion is what we feel when these changes in our bodies take place. The purpose of the count-to-ten time-out advice was to allow your epinephrine levels to subside and your state of physiological arousal to return to normal so that your feelings of anger would also subside.

As I noted in the last chapter, one of the effects of increased levels of epinephrine in the body is to stimulate activity in the brain and other parts of the nervous system. This effect will no doubt be appreciated by all the people who can not quite get into mental gear until they have had their morning cup of coffee or tea and taken in an artificial form of epinephrine, namely caffeine. With recent advances in our understanding of neurobiology, it is becoming increasingly evident that memory, which is clearly an activity of the nervous system, is enhanced by emotion through increased levels of epinephrine and other hormones that are released during an emotional state, as McGaugh states, "Findings of many experimental studies of humans as well as animal memory suggest that the emotional arousal induced by an experience is an important determinant of the strength of memory for the event" (McGaugh, 1995, p. 256).

In simpler times, this connection between emotional arousal and memory made perfect sense. When an event caused us to become emotionally and physically aroused it was an event that was important to remember for survival. It would be beneficial, for example, to have immediate and permanent memory for fear-provoking events so that they could be avoided in the future, or so that we could become immediately prepared to deal with them.

Witnessing a motor vehicle collision is an emotionally arousing event, but perhaps more so for the participants than for the bystanders. We might, therefore, expect someone who was involved and therefore more emotionally aroused, to have a better recollection of the collision than a bystander. In like fashion, we might expect an eyewitness who viewed a highly emotionally arousing event, such as a violent head-on crash, to have a better recollection than an eyewitness who viewed a more emotionally neutral event like a minor fender-bender.

The research available on this issue is somewhat indirect. Most of the studies dealing with emotion and recollection are related to criminal events rather than to traffic events. One issue which has been studied has been labeled *weapon focus*, from the belief that victims of crimes in which a weapon is present tend to narrow their focus of attention to the weapon. This results in enhanced attention to weapon details but reduced attention to other details such as the perpetrator and the scene. This notion is supported by a number of studies (Johnson and Scott, 1976; Kramer, Buckout and Eugenio, 1990; Loftus, Loftus and Messo, 1987; Maas and Kohnken, 1989). These data appear to be consistent with the related finding reported earlier that central details of the scene appear to be more resistant to the effects of misinformation than peripheral details (Loftus, 1996). Presumably, I suspect, they involved more focused attention and were thus more likely to be remembered accurately in their original form.

The question, then, of whether emotional arousal is likely to enhance memory for a witness to a motor vehicle collision is both yes and no. It is likely that emotional arousal will lead to better recollection of original events that were central to the individual's attention at the time of the events, and lead to worse recollection of original events that were peripheral to the individual's focus of attention. Thus, a driver may have a fairly veridical recollection of the vehicle on which he was visually focused and with which he collided, but little or no recollection of other details at the scene. A more emotionally neutral witness, such as a bystander, may provide better recollection of peripheral details than a highly emotionally aroused driver or passenger.

Performance of subjects on a variety of tasks has been shown to exhibit a slightly more complex relationship than that just described by the weapon focus research. The relationship was first described by Yerkes and Dodson (1908) and came to be known as the Yerkes-Dodson law. The law states that at very low levels of arousal, learning and performance are correspondingly low but they increase as the level of arousal increases up to a point, beyond which any further increases in arousal reduce learning and performance. The relationship is best described as an upside down u-shaped function in which the maximum levels of learning and performance occur at moderate levels of arousal and the lowest levels of learning and performance are found at both very low and very high levels of arousal. The ideal level of arousal will of course vary from individual to individual, but will also vary with the familiarity of the task for the individual. A simple task which is well learned will be more resistant to the effects of high arousal than will be a complex or unfamiliar task. Loftus (1996) describes this phenomenon as follows: In a moment of intense fear a person would probably still be able to spell his name, but his ability to play a good game of chess would be seriously impaired.

The relationship between learning and performance on the one hand, and emotional arousal on the other, may have implications for the formation of memory of witnesses at the scene as well as for the witness's later recollections. The Yerkes-Dodson law would predict that at the scene, information will be most effectively processed by those who are experiencing moderate levels of arousal and who are most familiar with the types of events that have occurred. On this basis, bystanders, who presumably have somewhat lower arousal levels than involved persons, would be in the best position to process the events that take place during a collision, especially if the scene and situations are familiar to them. Highly emotionally aroused persons, such as drivers and occupants, would be least likely to effectively process the collision information in general.

Additionally, the Yerkes-Dodson law would predict that witnesses who are attempting to recall the events surrounding the collision would perform better under moderately arousing conditions, particularly if the information to be recollected has been well practiced or rehearsed. A courtroom can be an intimidating context for novice witnesses to recall what happened at the scene of a collision. Levels of emotional arousal are likely to be very high in those that find a courtroom unfamiliar. These levels of arousal can interfere with the witness's ability to recall and to process new or complex information. To maximize the witness's ability to recall and to think in a courtroom setting, it would be prudent to ensure that the witness is well rehearsed. This will have the effect of increasing the optimum level of arousal for the witness. Additionally it should be effective to familiarize the witness with both the courtroom setting as well as the procedures that he or she will encounter in order to keep the level of arousal from going beyond the optimum level when the recollection takes place.

Memory, we have seen, is a complex issue. Though it may be reasonably faithful at the sensory level in terms of the original events, and very nearly veridical for those events that were processed at the short-term memory level, beyond that, during the transition to long-term memory, it is dynamic and ever-changing, incomplete and subject to distortion by a myriad of influences. Eyewitness memory is much like a patchwork quilt made up of individual swatches of perception. Some swatches are initially acquired while others are left behind. Over time the retained swatches are examined, some modified, some even discarded and replaced by new ones. Finally, though, the swatches are sewn together, bound by the threads of unshakable confidence, to form a final memory for the collision that is reported to the triers of fact.

Clearly, any evidence bearing on a motor vehicle collision case which is as malleable as human recollection deserves considerable caution. As eyewitnesses to motor vehicle collisions people do not, for the most part, seek to deceive. Memories of the events surrounding a collision represent a synthesis of what was originally attended to and observed, what made logical sense to the witness at the time of the memory formation, and the beliefs and discoveries made by the witness between the time of the original events and the time that they are reported.

In this chapter we have explored some of the frailties of human memory as they relate to the ability of the eyewitness to faithfully process and retain the events of a motor vehicle collision. In the next chapter we will explore what kinds of processes can prevent the witness from recalling from memory the events that were successfully retained, whether faithful to the original observations or not.

Chapter 4

Forgetting:
Forgotten but Not Lost?

A few years ago, my wife and I were dining out when my attention was captured by a woman with her dining companion seated several tables away from us. The woman looked remarkably familiar to both of us but neither I nor my wife could place her exactly. As fate would have it, the next morning I was walking from the subway to my office at the university, and as was my custom I took a shortcut through a commercial retail complex which housed our dentist's office. As I neared the dentist's office it hit me like a ton of bricks. The woman we had noticed the evening before was our dentist's receptionist. I was suddenly struck by a flood of recollection. I could now clearly see her face in my mind and remember her name, and I could picture her sitting behind the reception counter. I could have provided, if you had asked me at that moment, a wealth of detail about her appearance and mannerisms. Perhaps you have had a similar experience involving a chance encounter with an old acquaintance out of the normal context. Such experiences always serve to remind me that often, forgetting is not as much about losing information as it is about failing to locate it at a particular moment in time. More formally, forgetting means the inability to remember, retrieve or recall a previously retained experience or event. Forgetting can mean different things, depending on the depth or level at which the information was initially retained.

This leads us to an important axiom: You can not remember what you never consciously processed in the first place. This seems like such an obvious statement that it is easy to miss the significance of the message. Though we often use the term much more loosely than we ought, forgetting requires that there was a previous memory. Have you ever been at a party and while being introduced to someone you were mentally so busy processing the individual's features or so distracted by the presence of someone else in the room that you missed the details of the introduction altogether? This is a common embarrassing moment for most of us and while we say that we have forgotten who we were just introduced to, what we really mean is that we never actually processed the information in the first place and therefore never truly formed a memory of the event. While this may seem like nitpicking to some, it is in fact an important distinction to make. When an eyewitness says, "Gee, I forget," or "I can't remember," in response to a question, it creates the impression that the witness did at least process the information at the outset, and for whatever reason, he or she is unable to retrieve it at the present moment. This is very different from the impression that is formed when an eyewitness says, "Gee, I never saw that," or "I never heard that." Because we fail to make this distinction between forgetting and lack of initial processing in our own everyday lives, we usually don't challenge others to make it either. We may thus get a false impression about how much detail an eyewitness actually processed in the first place.

4.1 Forgetting in Sensory Memory and Short-Term Memory

In sensory memory, information which is not immediately transferred to short-term memory is lost or forgotten in a matter of seconds. Here, at least, the term *lost* is quite appropriate since if the information is not selected for additional processing it is quite literally gone forever. As was discussed earlier, the sensory register can handle large amounts of information, but they are retained for only a brief instant in time unless processed further at the level of short-term memory. Forgetting in sensory memory occurs due to decay of the memory traces themselves. In short-term memory, some of the information that is processed at this level may decay and some of the information may be displaced. Recall that in short term memory there are both capacity and duration limits. Capacity is limited to about seven chunks of information and duration is limited to about thirty seconds without rehearsal. If we attempt to process more than seven chunks of information, then any additional information will have to displace some of the existing information that is already in short-term memory.

You might think of short-term memory in terms of an upper bookshelf that is capable of holding about seven books. Imagine that each book will remain on the shelf for about thirty seconds after which it falls to the floor and is lost to you. Below that bookshelf is an enormous lower shelf that will hold all the books you wish, and from which the books can not fall. If you attempt to place an eighth book on the upper shelf it will not fit and you will have to remove one of the existing books to make room for it. Of course, if you wait long enough some of the books will fall off anyway and room will be created. If you want to keep a book shelved longer than thirty seconds you will have to voluntarily remove it and place it on the lower permanent shelf. Occasionally, a book will fall off the seven-book shelf and land on the lower shelf where it will remain. Additionally, you can catch a falling book before it hits the floor and place it back on the seven-book shelf for another thirty seconds.

Short-term memory works something like the book shelves. Information is processed and retained automatically for about thirty seconds with a limitation of about seven chunks of information. If you process a particular chunk of information no further, then after about thirty seconds it will decay and be lost forever (the falling books). With rehearsal (catching the books and putting them back on the shelf) you can keep the information cycling through short-term memory and occasionally some of it will be stored permanently in long-term memory (some of the falling books will accidentally land on the lower shelf during their fall). Some information can be deliberately processed at a deeper level and thus transferred to long term memory (voluntary removal and placement on the lower shelf). When the rate of presentation of information exceeds the seven chunk capacity of short-term memory, it will displace information already in short-term memory (removing a book to make room for a new one) and the displaced information will be lost. Thus, forgetting in short-term memory may result from decay over time or from displacement due to the information's having exceeded the seven chunk limit and produced overload.

4.2 Forgetting in Long-Term Memory

Once information is processed deeply enough to constitute long-term memory, it is thought not to decay. Earlier I suggested that there were no real practical limits on either the capacity or duration of long-term memory. At the beginning of this chapter I described a personal experience in which I was unable to recall the identity of the receptionist at my dentist's office until the next day following our chance meeting. Such experiences suggest that sometimes the information is not really forgotten, but instead is temporarily inaccessible. Forgetting in long-term memory is mostly the inability to lo-cate or retrieve information which is still retained or stored. This can happen for a variety of reasons.

4.3 Cue-Dependent Forgetting

When information, such as a description of my dentist's receptionist, is placed in long-term memory, it is organized and stored according to its as-sociation to existing information. For example, the receptionist description might be linked to a description of my dentist, to the features of his office, or to the retail building housing the office and to other people working there. These other bits of information act as retrieval cues or triggers for the recall of the receptionist information. When I encountered her outside of her nor-mal context, none of the necessary cues were available, so the random search for the needed information was unsuccessful. This type of forgetting has thus been called *cue-dependent forgetting*. Of course the next day as I walked through the office complex and passed the dentist's office, the correct cues were encountered which triggered the receptionist information and a flood of information linked to those cues. This type of forgetting explains why it is difficult to recognize people with whom we have become familiar in one setting, but are then encountered in a new setting.

Related to this notion is the idea that recollection is often improved or forgetting minimized by attempting to recall information in the same setting in which the information was originally learned or processed. The obvious effect of this would be to make available all the retrieval cues that were associated with the learned material at the time that it was processed. The implication of this notion is that if you want to maximize the amount of recollection and minimize the amount of forgetting for an eyewitness, he or she should be interviewed at the collision scene.

4.4 State-Dependent Forgetting

It has been demonstrated that people have more difficulty remembering something if they are asked to recall it in a different emotional or physiologi-cal state than that in which the information was originally processed (Bower, 1981; Weingartner et al., 1977). It is a common enough experience for can-didates to tense up during a job interview or for students to become overly anxious during an exam and discover that they blank out and forget what they knew or learned during their preparation for the event. Then they find that as soon as they leave the job interview or test setting and begin to relax that all that they had wished to recall earlier but had temporarily forgotten now returns in a torrent of free flowing memory. While too late to do the job candidates and students any good now, it arrives just in time to demonstrate to us that a physiological or emotional change can produce forgetting in long-term memory. This type of forgetting is called *state-dependent forgetting*. It can be minimized if the state of arousal during the original processing of the information and the state of arousal during the recall of the information are matched. Both the job applicant and the student likely prepared for their respective ordeals in a state of relative relaxation. We might, therefore, teach them strategies that would help them relax during their respective trials in order to minimize this type of forgetting. This is a relevant effect for consideration of the eyewitness. It suggests that the extent to which the state of arousal under which the original collision was observed matches the state during which recall takes place, will determine to some degree how much and how accurately the original observations will be recalled. In the previous chapter I discussed the potential effect that emotional arousal might have on eyewitness memory with respect to central versus peripheral details of the collision. I also introduced the Yerkes-Dodson law which described witness memory as a potential function of level of arousal with moderate arousal levels offering the optimum conditions for both memory and recall. Very high or very low levels of arousal should impede the performance of the witness. Compared to these effects, the effect of matching the witness's physiological or emotional state under recall conditions to the state under which the events of the collision were originally processed is probably quite small. Nonetheless, a number of small effects can have a cumulative effect and should not be ignored.

4.5 Interference

Frequently we encounter situations in which something we have previously learned can make it more difficult to learn something new, and in which newly acquired information can make it more difficult to recall something previously learned. In other words some information, whether new or old, interferes with either the acquisition or recollection of other information. These effects are called *proactive interference* and *retroactive interference* respectively.

Proactive interference acts forward in time so that old information interferes with new information. Someone who has first learned to water ski will undoubtedly find it harder to learn to downhill ski on snow than will a person who has learned neither previously. In water skiing one needs to learn to lean back, while in downhill skiing one needs to learn to keep the weight forward. Water skiers discover that old habits die hard and their previously learned tendency to lean back interferes with their ability to learn how to downhill ski. Eyewitnesses who are exposed to new information, but who have already formed a strong impression or memory of the collision may be unable to accommodate new and important information. Bartlett (1932) demonstrated that when people are asked to process information and later to recollect that information on repeated occasions, initial memories for the events can be substantially inaccurate but equally importantly, those inaccurate memories are highly persistent over time. Loftus (1996) describes the relevance of the effect for our purposes this way, "[I]f a witness to an accident reports early on that the driver of the damaged vehicle ran a red light, this detail would be likely to appear in later recollections, whether it was true or not" (p. 84). Thus it would appear that an observation previously acquired and well entrenched in the initial memory for the event is highly resistant to change in light of new, and perhaps more accurate, information.

Retroactive interference acts backward in time so that newly acquired information can make it more difficult to accurately recall previously learned information. Frequently, immigrants who assimilate into a new culture and acquire the language of the new culture discover that after some time, many of the words of their former vocabularies are forgotten and they have to relearn parts of their native languages. An eyewitness who interacts with other people at the scene of a collision may acquire new information. This new information may interfere with the ability to recall the original observations of the collision.

4.6 Amnesia

Amnesia refers to the type of forgetting that is associated with brain injury or physical or emotional trauma. It may result either from the inability of the nervous system to process new information or from the inability to retrieve previously stored information. It is common enough in motor vehicle collisions, especially those involving severe impacts and high levels of personal injury, for some of the occupants to report being unable to remember some of the events surrounding the collision. In *retrograde amnesia* the person has difficulty remembering events that occurred prior to the trauma, while in *anterograde amnesia* the individual reports difficulty remembering events that took place following the trauma. Memory loss in amnesiac witnesses would not be expected to be random. The degree of memory loss is usually a function of time—the closer in time to the traumatic event one examines the memory loss, the greater it is likely to be. Thus, an individual may have a recollection of events well before or well after the traumatic event but little or no recollection for events that occurred in close temporal proximity to the trauma. Additionally, the memory loss may be temporary, and as memories return they are likely to return first for events remote from the trauma and last for events close to the trauma.

An eyewitness who has sustained neurological injury or who has been subjected to extreme emotional or physiological trauma will be at a substantial disadvantage in his or her recollection of the events leading up to a collision. Recollection may return slowly in bits and pieces, beginning with events remote from the trauma inducing event, or, in the case of severe or extensive brain injury, perhaps not at all.

Forgetting can take on a number of different meanings, depending on the context and the type of memory that is involved. When a witness says, "I don't remember what happened," it could mean that he or she never actually observed the event; it could mean that he or she never processed the information beyond the level of sensory memory; it could mean that the information was lost from short-term memory before the witness had a chance to process it deeper for long-term retention; or it could mean that the information is still retained in long-term memory but for any number of possible reasons, including interference, missing cues, or neurological damage or disruption, is not retrievable at present. All of this suggests that as investigators, we need to probe witnesses more thoroughly in this aspect to seek more specific information regarding the source of the forgetting.

Chapter 5

Good Science: From the Ivory Tower to the Real World

Until now, we have examined a number of issues regarding eyewitness reliability, which all point to the need for caution when weighing the value of eyewitness recollection. At this point we need to consider what, if anything, this research can teach us about the behavior of real eyewitnesses in the world of the collision investigator or reconstructionist. To appreciate the meaning and practical implications of this research we first need to briefly examine some general scientific issues. Later, in Chapter 6, I will present the practical implications of the eyewitness research to the reconstruction and legal communities.

5.1 The Scientific Model

The scientific model is one of many approaches to understanding the world around us. There are other ways of understanding the world, such as religion and philosophy, that we will not examine here. The goals of any scientific inquiry are to describe, to predict, to explain or understand, and to control the behavior of the variables of interest. A variable is simply any characteristic which can take on a number of values, depending on the situation. It is the opposite of a constant, which always keeps the same value. In collision reconstruction we treat the acceleration due to gravity, g, as a constant and assign it a value for earthbound vehicles of 9.81 m/sec/sec (32.2 ft/sec/sec). The distance traveled by a skidding vehicle would be a variable. That is, it would change or vary with the speed of the vehicle, the nature of the surface over which the vehicle is sliding, the composition of the tires, and so forth. The ultimate goal of science is to discover how variables are related so that we understand how one variable affects or influences another, and thus gain control over those variables. To accomplish this, scientists must be able to distinguish cause variables from effect variables in the events that they observe.

Much of the research in eyewitness reliability has come from the field of psychology and related disciplines. The scientific value of any piece of research can be measured along two dimensions. The first is the ability of the research effort to isolate cause and effect relationships so that we have convincing evidence that one variable is responsible for the other. The second is the ability of the research to extend its results to the real world and to the population and situations of interest in that world.

5.2 Internal Validity

The mere fact that two variables are related to one another does not necessarily mean that one causes the other. It is likely that in your town or city there is a strong positive relationship between the softness of the asphalt on the roadways and soft drink sales, which is, as the asphalt gets softer, soft drink sales increase. These variables are related to one another or correlated in a predictable fashion. Yet, few people would be foolish enough to invest heavily in soft drink company stock, purchase a blow torch, and set about to soften the asphalt on the roadways in order to make a profit on their investments. Sometimes, as in this example, we have an intuitive understanding that just because two variables are correlated doesn't mean that one is the cause of the other. Clearly, both the softness of the asphalt and soft drink sales are causally related to a third variable, ambient temperature, which, as it rises, produces an increase in both of the others. Sometimes the relationship is not so obvious as to cause and effect, and we need to rely on scientific principles and methodology to distinguish such relationships for us. To the extent that a research study is able to isolate cause and effect relationships between the variables of interest, we say that the study has internal validity.

In the universe around us things are continually in flux; it is a world of never ending change. In such a world it is useful to be able to predict certain changes. While we might enjoy a natural change of weather, we prefer a predictable change so that we can plan our lives effectively and safely by arranging our wearing apparel and our activities appropriately. It would be somewhat inconvenient to have to carry an umbrella everyday just in case it might rain. We would much rather carry one only on days when a high likelihood of rain exists. Thus, we want to be able to predict which days carry the highest likelihood of rain and tote the umbrella only on those days. Ideally, though, we would prefer to be able to control rather than simply predict the weather. That way, rather than merely adjust our behavior to suit the weather, we could adjust the weather to suit our purposes.

The first step in controlling any variable is understanding what other things influence or affect it. The variable which is being influenced is known as the *dependent variable*, since it depends for its value on the influence of something else. The variable which is causing changes in the dependent variable is called the *independent variable*. You can think of the independent variable as the cause-variable and the dependent variable as the effect-variable. Suppose you were interested in knowing whether the installation of antilock brake systems (ABS) on vehicles could reduce the braking distance required for a vehicle. You would have to compare a group of vehicles equipped with ABS to a group of vehicles without ABS. For each group you would have to measure the braking distance. In this example, the type of braking system would constitute the independent variable and the braking distance would constitute the dependent variable. The braking distance should vary with the presence or absence of ABS if the two variables are related.

Suppose further that you found six vehicles (two Cadillac DeVilles, three Chevrolet Caprices, and one Crown Victoria) that had ABS and six vehicles (two Toyota Corollas, one Chevrolet Sprint, and three Ford Escorts) without. You realize that since braking distance is a function of speed, you will have to skid the vehicles from the same initial speed. You have the test drivers accelerate each of the twelve vehicles to exactly 30 m.p.h. on a dry asphalt track and brake as hard as they can. You measure the braking distance for each vehicle and calculate the averages for each of the ABS and non-ABS groups. You find that the ABS group required an average of 36 ft to stop while the non-ABS group required an average of 39 ft to stop. Did the presence or absence of ABS affect the stopping distance? Your inclination might be to say Yes, it reduced braking distance by an average of 3 ft. Clearly the ABS group outperformed the non-ABS group, but was it the ABS that caused the difference or might there have been other differences between the groups that would explain the results?

5.3 Control

The vehicle model types that you employed in the ABS study were very different between the two groups. It is possible that the ABS group had stickier tires on average than the other group, or shorter brake lag times, or different weight shift characteristics. Perhaps the more expensive ABS group of cars might have out performed the inexpensive non-ABS group even if the ABS models had not been equipped with ABS. You slowly begin to realize that there are potentially many differences between the two groups besides the presence or absence of ABS, any one of which might explain the difference in braking distance. To rule out other possible explanations for the results of the study you would have to exert sufficient control over all the variables, that only two variables are allowed to change, the independent variable, controlled by you, and the dependent variable. All other variables, usually referred to as *extraneous variables*, are held constant. *Control* in a study refers to the ability of the researcher to allow only the variables of interest to change, and thus eliminate any alternate explanations for the results.

To properly test whether ABS affects braking distance, the two groups would have to be absolutely identical except for just one thing: the only difference that can exist is that one group has ABS and the other does not. The ideal way to execute such a study would be to run each of the ABS equipped vehicles twice, once with the ABS system activated and once with the ABS system deactivated. Each vehicle would act as its own control in the deactivated condition, ensuring that all possible characteristics, other than ABS, are the same in both test conditions. This way, if the same difference in stopping distance were measured, the difference could only be attributable to activation of the ABS and nothing else. As a final caution, you would have to *counterbalance* the order of your runs so that about half the time the ABS-on condition is performed first and about half the time the ABS-off condition appears first. The reason for this is that it could happen that cold brakes behave differently from hot brakes, or cold tires differently from hot ones and so on. Reversing the order for each run would prevent any order effects from influencing the results when the results are averaged.

If you did all this and still obtained shorter average stopping distances for the ABS condition, then you could be reasonably confident that there was a cause and effect relationship between the presence of ABS and stopping distances. You will have demonstrated that the application of ABS causes shorter stopping distances.

5.4 The Role of Chance

Even if you did everything right and controlled all possible variables, could you still be absolutely sure of the result? Could the ABS group have stopped shorter on average than the non-ABS vehicles due to chance alone? After all, bizarre chance events do occur in our world. People do get struck by lightning and people do win lotteries in spite of the staggering odds against these events. Scientists can never really know, for sure, whether the results of their particular studies were due to the manipulation of their independent variables or due to chance, but they can reduce the likelihood of chance-produced results by repeating their studies, especially if the study is repeated by other independent investigators. When a study is repeated and produces the same results each time, the results are said to be consistent or *reliable*. To the extent that the same relationship can be demonstrated on a variety of occasions and by a variety of researchers, the research demonstrating that relationship is said to be reliable.

A very special way of determining reliability is through the use of statistical analysis. The field of statistics is essentially based on the notion that while we can never be certain whether a particular experimental event was the result of chance or the result of a relationship between the variables, we can determine the frequency that the event would be produced by chance if only chance were at work. By comparing the actual test results to that which would be expected if only chance were working, the researcher can determine the probability that his or her test results were due to chance. This is referred to as the *level of significance* or *statistical significance* of a test result. The lower the probability that a result was produced by chance, the greater the likelihood that the results were produced by something other than chance, such as the systematic and meaningful relationship between the variables. These probabilities are usually expressed as a proportional value of one.

As an example, imagine that the results of the ABS study described earlier were statistically analyzed with the result that the probability was less than .01 ($p < .01$) that chance produced the difference of three feet between the average stopping distance of the ABS vehicles and the average stopping distance of the non-ABS vehicles. This means that chance alone would produce the observed difference less than one time in one hundred trials. Another way of stating this result is that if you repeated the study one hundred times, a difference in stopping distance of three feet should only happen once by chance alone. Now, while chance might have produced this one result it is considerably unlikely. This level of statistical significance gives us confidence that our result is due to a relationship between ABS and stopping distance, not due to chance, and by claiming that ABS produced the difference in stopping distance we will, on average, only be wrong one time in a hundred or less.

5.5 Statistical Significance versus Usefulness

The fact that a particular experimental outcome is statistically significant does not necessarily mean that the result is useful. Consider the outcome of our fictitious ABS study in which the ABS-equipped vehicles stopped three feet sooner than the non-ABS vehicles. While the result was statistically significant and could only occur by chance one time or less in a hundred trials on average, the actual difference in stopping distance might not be of any practical importance. As another example, consider that a scientist has discovered a cold remedy which he believes will shorten the duration of a cold for its users. Before he can market it he must test its effectiveness on a clinical sample. Let us assume for a moment that he has administered the remedy to a group of cold sufferers in a properly conceived and conducted experiment and discovers that as a result, the group of cold sufferers that took the remedy recovered from their colds an average of twelve minutes sooner than the group that did not receive the remedy. This difference of twelve minutes was statistically significant, that is, it is highly unlikely that the difference was due to chance and very likely due to the medication. It is difficult to imagine a large group of people lining up at their local pharmacies to pay for a cold remedy that will shorten the duration of their colds by only twelve minutes!

The practical significance or usefulness of much of the eyewitness research is rather difficult to assess. For example, in the Loftus and Palmer (1974) study cited earlier, subjects were asked to estimate the speed of colliding vehicles. Subjects received different verbal descriptions of the impact, ranging from "contacted" to "smashed" which resulted in about a 10 mph speed estimate difference between these two extremes. This result was statistically significant in the actual study, demonstrating that the difference in speed estimates was likely due to the verbal description of the impact, rather than to chance. Does this experimental result have any practical significance? Would the fact that witnesses could vary in their speed estimates by as much as 10 mph affect the actual outcome of a specific real-world case? The answer to these questions would, of course, be dependent on the particulars of the case at hand; such a difference might or might not alter the outcome of any particular case.

Generally, the scientific studies in the area of eyewitness reliability as reported here have demonstrated sufficient statistical reliability that the only unanswered issue is that of practical importance. If the decisive issue in a particular case were the correct identification of a driver, for example, then a single instance of mistaken identification would be catastrophic. It is paramount, therefore, that any scientific evidence that reliably delineates a potential failure in any aspect of eyewitness recollection in the laboratory be considered to have potential practical significance as well.

5.6 External Validity

Internal validity is the hallmark of good science, but it comes with a price. Often, the only way to achieve internal validity is through careful control of all the variables at hand. The only way to achieve absolute control over variables is to work in a laboratory-like setting, far removed from the real world. Much of the research on eyewitness reliability is high in internal validity, as it is carefully constructed, and executed in a laboratory setting in order to maximize control over the variables, and ensure that cause and effect relationships are isolated. Unfortunately, the further away we get from the real world, the less likelihood there is that the study will be applicable to the real population and situations of interest. Much of the research done by Loftus and her colleagues was performed using undergraduate psychology students at the University of Washington as subjects, since they were most readily available and cost-effective. The question remains whether we can reasonably generalize the results from young university students in a relatively calm emotional state to the eyewitness population in general. To the extent that a study employs subjects, procedures, and conditions that are like those that would be experienced in the real world, the study is said to have *external validity*.

Recall the imaginary ABS study. Since we exerted maximum control over the variables, then we are pretty sure that we isolated ABS as the cause and skid distance as the effect. What can we say from the results of this study? Can we say that all ABS equipped vehicles will produce shorter stopping distances under all conditions? No we can not. We didn't test all ABS equipped vehicles and we didn't test all possible conditions. All that we are really justified in saying is that, at least for the vehicles tested and for the road surface conditions tested, the relationship holds. To discover whether it holds for other vehicles, other tire types, other speeds, or other road conditions, we would have to conduct additional tests. You can see from this why good science advances as slowly as it does.

External validity is achieved by choosing subjects and conditions that match the subjects and conditions of real interest and by subjecting them to procedures that match what they might actually encounter in real life. For example, if you were interested in knowing whether it is possible to change witness's memories of a collision by exposing them to misleading post-event information, you might attend a real accident scene, pretend that you were a witness, and relate to the real witnesses some misleading piece of information. Afterward, you could examine the witness statements to see if any of them incorporated your misleading information into their memory of the events. If you were successful then it would be clear that the effect is applicable to real eyewitnesses in the real world.

Unfortunately, studies which are high in external validity tend to place subjects in a position of potential harm and can not be performed by scientists unless strict safeguards are employed to protect participants from psychological, emotional, or physical detriment. One of the important safeguards generally employed by scientists that use human subjects in their experiments is informed consent. Here, all the potential risks must be explained to the subjects prior to their involvement, and their subsequent participation must be clearly voluntary with an opportunity afforded them for withdrawal of their participation at any time during the study.

Because real collisions are generally traumatic events, such ethical considerations have impeded the transition of knowledge about eyewitnesses from the laboratory to the real world. We can not experimentally subject people to real collisions and so we can not obtain the same degree of reality that actual drivers, occupants, and bystanders would experience in a naturally occurring event. On the other hand, we do not know for certain if this makes any difference. We can suppose that there is a difference for participants between a real-world collision and a staged collision, but we have no way of finding out if it is so.

Much of the scientific work on driver perception-response times has used informed or at least partially informed individuals as the subject drivers. These drivers may not know exactly what they will encounter but they no doubt suspect that something will happen and may be in a state of hyperreadiness during the reaction trials. It is likely that because they are prepared for something, their reaction times are shorter than would be the case if they were not aware that they were being studied. If we were not bounded by ethical guidelines we might secret ourselves along a busy highway and place stuffed animals or human mannequins or some such items on the roadway or drive in front of other vehicles and brake hard and observe driver reaction times in the real world. The potential for harm is rather obvious in these cases, demonstrating why it is that science often has to settle for experimental designs which have greater control (more internal validity) but which are less applicable to the real world of interest (less external validity).

Most of the eyewitness reliability studies that I have reported here have extended the experimental procedures as far as ethical considerations will allow, in order to provide the maximum amount of generalization from the results. For example, in the Maas and Köhnken (1989) study on weapon focus that I reported in Chapter 3, the investigators could not have the experimental confederate brandishing a gun to unsuspecting subjects. They realized that for most subjects a hypodermic syringe combined with the belief that they might be subjected to its use could be sufficiently emotionally stimulating to produce the desired effect. Whether the observed effect was close to what would have been achieved had a real gun been used is anybody's guess; we have no way of determining what, if any, differences would exist between the two procedures.

Science is therefore limited in how far it can go to determine the applicability of a particular experimental outcome. I don't envision a relaxation of the ethical rules for scientific inquiry in the future; I suspect we have gone just about as far as ethics will allow. Within the ethical boundaries set for it, it appears that the scientific community has done a fairly compelling job of isolating some critical concerns with respect to eyewitness reliability. While you may subscribe to the notion that the nature of the subjects and procedures used in the eyewitness research doesn't exactly match the real world, this may not be a necessary condition to cause concern for the results and their ensuing application in the real world.

Chapter 6

Some Practical Considerations: Pick Me Up and Dust Me Off

═══

Synopsis
6.1 What We See and Hear Are Products of Our Minds, Not of Our Eyes and Ears
6.2 People Are Very Poor Judges of Vehicle Distances and Speeds
6.3 Eyewitnesses Consistently Overestimate the Time Duration of Events
6.4 The Phrase "I Don't Remember" May Mean Different Things for Different Witnesses
6.5 Human Memory Is Not like a Recording Device
6.6 Memory Is Autobiographical in Nature
6.7 Memory Is Not Stable Over Time
6.8 Our Memories Can Become Distorted
6.9 People Are Overconfident in Their Recollections
6.10 The Legal System Places More Trust in Eyewitness Evidence Than Is Justified
6.11 Emotion Facilitates Improved Memory for Central Events but Poorer Memory for Peripheral Events
6.12 Some Concluding Remarks

Pure science is not necessarily intended to improve our daily existence; its primary goal is the advancement of knowledge. Every once in a while, however, some advances do impact our mundane lives. The field of eyewitness reliability is one of those cases where scientific initiative was prompted by a societal need. Thus, each step that we have taken toward a better understanding of the fragility of human recollection could lead directly to changes in the legal processes that are designed to serve and protect us and as such, harbor the potential to affect each and every one of us.

The thoughtful and often provocative research designs used by Elizabeth Loftus and her followers represent science at its best: highly controlled studies that stretched experimental procedures to their ethical limits and led to reliable findings of great practical importance. Often, scientific endeavors serve to validate our sense of the way the world works, in an expected but nonetheless important way. Occasionally, however, scientific results refute our general understanding and serve to alter our beliefs dramatically. In this chapter I summarize, from the findings discussed earlier in this book, what I believe to be the most significant characteristics of human recollection and eyewitness reliability for the practitioner. Some of these will be consistent with our own life experiences, but others may run contrary to some basic beliefs that we hold.

6.1 What We See and Hear Are Products of Our Minds, Not of Our Eyes and Ears

Optical illusions and other phenomena demonstrate in a rather dramatic fashion that we don't always see and hear what actually exists. As our minds attempt to interpret the information that is streaming through the senses we can be easily misled about and can misconstrue important events. Often we see and hear what we want or expect to happen rather than what is actually out there. Seeing, hearing, feeling, smelling and tasting are subjective and interpretive events that depend not only on what the senses are processing at the time but equally importantly, on the lifetime of experience that we bring to the witnessing situation and on our immediate needs, expectations, and desires.

6.2 People Are Very Poor Judges of Vehicle Distances and Speeds

In spite of a myriad of cues available to the brain by which to judge distances and speeds of other moving vehicles and objects, people perform very poorly in this regard, particularly for very small objects like motorcycles, and very large objects like trains. Additionally, our judgements of objective quantities like speed and distance can be dramatically affected by our subjective perceptions of the context. An excellent example of this was found in the Loftus and Palmer (1974) study in which subjects' speed estimations for colliding vehicles was rather strikingly influenced by the description of the collision in spite of the fact that they all viewed the same collision. Drivers generally rely on proximity of other vehicles rather than judgements of speed and distance in making decisions about whether to proceed into traffic.

6.3 Eyewitnesses Consistently Overestimate the Time Duration of Events

When people observe events and then attempt to estimate their duration, they typically overestimate the time that those events took. This phenomenon is both consistent and powerful, and has implications not only for the eyewitness who misperceives the time duration, but for the jury evaluating the eyewitness testimony as well. People generally fail to comprehend the brevity of the events surrounding a collision which take place quite literally in the blink of an eye.

6.4 The Phrase "I Don't Remember" May Mean Different Things for Different Witnesses

Memory can only exist for events that were consciously attended to initially. Witnesses can not be expected to remember events to which they never attended and therefore never consciously processed in the first place. It is important to draw a distinction between the witness who says, "I don't remember," to mean, "I never actually processed that event and stored it in memory," and the witness who uses the same phrase, but means, "I did process that event and store it in memory but can't retrieve it from memory at this particular moment."

6.5 Human Memory Is Not like a Recording Device

Human memory is a product of human perception. Perception is a unique and personal interpretation of the events that occur around us, not a literal representation of them. Unlike a video camera which records everything visible in front of the lens, human attention is directed to parts of the scene that are relevant to the individual at a particular point in time. Unlike a camera lens which is essentially fixed, the human eyes are constantly in motion focusing on different parts of the scene at different times, based on the individual's perception about what is personally important and what is not. The camera does not make such judgements. The video camera captures whatever passes in front of the lens, whether interesting or not, whether important or not, but human memory captures only that which the eyes focus on and which the human observer deems important enough to attend to and to process.

6.6 Memory Is Autobiographical in Nature

What we focus on, and therefore what we actually process, will depend to a large extent on what our own experience tells us is worthwhile. To some extent we can liken memory for witnessed events to the making of a movie, in which the movie director is the eyewitness and the movie camera acts as the eyewitness's eyes. During the shooting of a movie the camera runs almost continuously but has only some of the actors and some of the scene in focus at any one time. The director must decide what to keep in focus and where to point the camera. If the director makes a mistake then an important part of the action may be lost. Likewise, the eyewitness must decide where in the collision scene to look and what to keep in focus. Inevitably, some of the scene will not be captured in memory. Unlike the movie director, however, the eyewitness can not request a retake. Ultimately, the movie director will have to decide what scenes of the many hours of film are important enough to keep, and much of the film will end up on the cutting room floor and never be viewed by the audience. In similar fashion, since the eyewitness can not process and store everything, much of the collision will not make it into memory. Our memory for the collision will be like the final screened version of the movie seen by audiences, from which scenes may have been deleted or to which scenes may have been added later. Just as the director discards scenes which are confusing and adds scenes that further the storytelling, so may eyewitnesses discard information which doesn't fit with their understanding and add information which allows what they have observed to make more sense overall.

6.7 Memory Is Not Stable Over Time

A video or audio recording is a relatively permanent storage medium, whereas human memory degrades quickly. Forgetting begins in less than one-half second for visual information and less than three seconds for auditory information. It follows a predictable pattern of loss which is not constant over time. Forgetting is rapid initially, with loss of about half of the material within the first hour following processing, and more gradually diminishing thereafter. Just as memory is selective, so is forgetting; what is forgotten first depends on the degree to which the individual was able to make sense of and organize the new information, and integrate it with existing knowledge. The less sensible and organized information, or information which is difficult to associate with existing memory, will be forgotten first.

6.8 Our Memories Can Become Distorted

Our recollections of witnessed events can be easily altered over time. As shown by the Loftus et al. studies, new information, whether true or false, can be introduced after the originally observed events and integrated into existing memory. While it is unclear from the research whether the new memories actually replace old ones or simply make them temporarily inaccessible, the new information is nonetheless retained as though it were the original memory. Therefore, we can never be sure whether a particular eyewitness recollection is original memory or altered memory. Unfortunately, memories do not have time-and-date stamps to alert us to when they were formed. Memory formation is a dynamic process not a static one. Over time we try to make sense of witnessed events. As we interact with other people and are exposed to new information, we begin to fill in the gaps inherent in our original memories and form new memories that replace the original memories. To the degree that our original memories have been changed or altered by subsequent ideas, inferences, and events, our memories have become distorted. This memory distortion is a natural and normal consequence of simply being human and none of us are exempt from these processes.

6.9 People Are Overconfident in Their Recollections

It is clear from the scientific literature that the degree of confidence a witness has in a particular recollection may bear no relationship to its accuracy. In our daily lives, we seldom test our specific recollections against reality since our memories usually serve a decision-making purpose and do not often have to be very specifically detailed. So long as we get the right meaning from things and events our memories generally serve us well. Outside of a legal context, people normally have no need for memories that act as perfect recording devices. Memories which process the essential meaning of things, but not every minute detail, are sufficient and lead us to become highly confident in our memory abilities. People are much more confident in their recollections of events than the level of detail inherent in their memory systems should permit. Once a memory has been formed, regardless of its accuracy, we become unshakably confident that it is so.

6.10 The Legal System Places More Trust in Eyewitness Evidence Than Is Justified

Jury members, attorneys and judges, are less critical of eyewitness testimony than the scientific literature has demonstrated that they ought to be. Additionally, eyewitnesses who demonstrate considerable confidence are judged to be more accurate and more credible than those exhibiting less confidence. Since the accuracy of the eyewitness is not necessarily related to the degree of confidence he or she has in his or her recollections, this judgement may well be in error. Even the most confident eyewitness may be mistaken in his or her recollections of a collision.

6.11 Emotion Facilitates Improved Memory for Central Events but Poorer Memory for Peripheral Events

Emotional arousal plays an important role in facilitating the physical events in the nervous system that are responsible for memory. Unfortunately, it appears that emotion produces a narrowing of the focus of attention. Thus, memory for important events which are central to the individual's focus of attention may benefit from emotional arousal while less salient and more peripheral details may go unnoticed. The literature on weapon focus demonstrated that emotional arousal generally improved eyewitness' recollection of central events, such as details of the weapon, while more peripheral details such as the physical appearance of the assailant were very poorly recalled. It also appears that emotional arousal is more beneficial to memory when the task and situation are familiar than when they are new or strange. Finally, moderate levels of emotional arousal are likely to result in optimal memory formation while very high and very low levels of arousal are less effective. Based on these findings, the ideal eyewitness would be familiar with the nature of collisions and be experiencing a moderate level of emotional arousal at the time that the collision was processed.

6.12 Some Concluding Remarks

While juries may still show a marked preference for eyewitness evidence over physical evidence, the physical evidence, when it exists, ought to be far more compelling. Physical evidence results from the natural laws of the universe and is inherently objective. No amount of wishing it to be so will shorten the tire marks left by a skidding vehicle or decrease the amount of kinetic energy and momentum that the vehicles bring into a collision. Eyewitness evidence, on the other hand, results from human memory and is inherently subjective in nature. As such, it is quite pliable and can be altered and changed over time. The same collision can be viewed by a number of different individuals and recollected differently by each. One of the hallmarks of a good scientific procedure is that it allows a number of different individuals to observe the same event and importantly, to draw the same conclusions from their observations. The use of eyewitness evidence to draw conclusions about the events surrounding the collision is very clearly not good science.

The time has come to enthusiastically challenge the notion that eyewitness evidence is inherently more valuable than physical evidence. Certainly there are circumstances that are appropriate for the use of eyewitness evidence. Some questions, such as, "Who had the green light?" can often not be answered by the physical evidence of a collision alone. Other collisions leave little or no useful physical evidence behind; here is plenty of grist for the eyewitness mill. When physical evidence does exist which is sufficient to answer all the questions of interest about the collision then do we really need eyewitness evidence at all? I believe that we do not. When physical evidence exists about a collision which leads to conclusions that are contrary to the eyewitness evidence, which should we believe? I believe that the physical evidence is far more compelling and should prevail.

A reliance on physical evidence rather than eyewitness evidence requires that collision investigators be sufficiently well trained and equipped to gather, interpret, and apply the physical traces of a collision to their investigations and to their conclusions. Technological advances such as total station surveying instruments, 3-D photogrammetry techniques, and so-called black boxes in air bag equipped vehicles make it increasingly likely in the future that useful physical evidence of collisions will be accessible to investigators who are well funded, well trained, and who are given sufficient time to gather and make use of the available physical evidence.

It is quite clear in my mind that the legal community and all those participating in the administration of justice ought to be educated about the unreliable nature of eyewitness evidence. Ordinary people, who may well be jury members some time in their lives, generally subscribe to a number of myths regarding the reliability of eyewitness evidence. In this book I have presented a number of scientifically established facts, many of which run counter to our normal perceptions and beliefs. Thus, many of the truths about eyewitness reliability are not within the normal range of knowledge for jury members. It is my ardent belief that if a legal case relies on eyewitness evidence, then an attempt ought to be made to educate all those involved on the relative strengths and weaknesses of physical and eyewitness evidence. The myths must first be dispelled before the jury members can properly apportion a weight to the eyewitness evidence in any particular case.

I have often thought that a court-appointed human factors expert might improve any particular trial situation by addressing the jury as a pretrial requirement. He or she could help ensure that each jury member brings to the proceedings a realistic and sufficient base of knowledge with which to evaluate the human evidence that will be heard.

Social scientists have been sounding their warnings regarding eyewitness reliability for several decades now; it is time we heeded those warnings. In eyewitness evidence there is no absolute truth; individual perception of truth is all there is.

References

Abel, T., Alberini, C., Ghirardi, M., Huang, Y., Nguyen, P., and Kandel, E. R. (1995) Steps toward a molecular definition of memory consolidation. In D.Schachter (Ed.) *Memory Distortion: How Minds, Brains, and Societies Reconstruct the Past.* U.S.A.: The President and Fellows of Harvard University.

Ainsworth, P.B. (1998) *Psychology, Law and Eyewitness Testimony.* Chichester: John Wiley & Sons.

Appleby, D. (1986) Déjà vu in the classroom. *Network*, 4, 8.

Bartlett, F.C. (1932) *Remembering: a study in experimental and social psychology.* New York: McMillan

Bower, G.H. (1981) Mood and memory. *American Psychologist*, 36: 129-148.

Buckout, R. (1984) Psychology of the eyewitness. In A. Pines and C. Maslach (Eds), *Experiencing Social Psychology: Readings and Projects.* New York: Alfred A. Knopf.

Bugelski, B.R. and Alampay, D.A. (1961) The role of frequency in developing perceptual sets. *Canadian Journal of Psychology*, **15**, 205-211.

Carlson, N. *(1990) Psychology the Science of Behavior* (3rd. Ed.). Toronto: Allyn & Bacon Craik, F. I. M. & Lockhart, R. S. (1972) Levels of processing: A framework for memory research. *Journal of Verbal Learning and Verbal Behavior*, 11, 671-684.

Craik, F. and Lockhart, R. (1972) Levels of Processing: A Framework for Memory Research. *Journal of Verbal Learning and Verbal Behavior*, 11, 671-684.

Festinger, L. (1957) *A Theory of Cognitive Dissonance.* Evanston, Il: Row, Peterson.

Fischbach, G.D. and Coyle, J.T. (1995) From the preface to Daniel L. Schacter (Ed.), *Memory Distortion.* U.S.A.: The President and Fellows of Harvard College.

Haber, R. N. and Haber, L. (2000) Experiencing, remembering and reporting events: the cognitive psychology of eyewitness testimony. *Psychology, Public Policy and Law*, 6, 1057-1097.

Harte, R.D. (1975) Estimates of the length of highway guidelines and spaces. *Human Factors*, 17, 455-460.

Huffman, K., Vernoy, M., Williams, B. and Vernoy, J. (1991) *Psychology in Action.* Toronto: John Wiley & Sons.

Johnson, C. and Scott, B. (1976) Eyewitness testimony and suspect identification as a function of arousal, sex of witness, and scheduling of interrogation. *Paper presented at the American Psychological Association*, Washington, D.C.

Kramer, T.H., Buckout, R. and Eugenio, P. (1990) Weapon focus, arousal, and eyewitness memory. *Law and Human Behavior*, 14, 167-184.

Loftus, E. F. (1975) Leading questions and the eyewitness report. *Cognitive Psychology*, 7, 560-572.

Loftus, E. F. (1977) Shifting human color memory. *Memory and Cognition*, 5, 696-699.

Loftus, E. F. (1996) *Eyewitness Testimony.* United States: President and Fellows of Harvard College.

Loftus, E.F. and Palmer, J.C. (1974) Reconstruction of automobile destruction: an example of the interaction between language and memory. *Journal of Verbal Learning* and Verbal Behavior, 13, 585-589.

Loftus, E. F., Loftus, G. R. and Messo, J. (1987) Some facts about "weapon focus". *Law and Human Behavior*, 11, 55-62.

Loftus, E. F., Miller, D. G., and Burns, H. J. (1978) Semantic integration of verbal information into visual memory. *Journal of Experimental Psychology: Human Learning and Memory.* 4, 1, 19-31.

Loftus, E.F., Schooler, J.W., Boones, S.M. and Kline, D. (1987) Time went by so slowly: Overestimation of event duration by males and females. *Applied Cognitive Psychology*, 1, 3-13.

Maas, A. and Köhnken, G. (1989) Eyewitness identification: Simulating the "weapon effect". *Law and Behavior*, 13, 397-408.

Mack, A. and Rock, I. (1998) *Inattentional Blindness.* Cambridge, Mass.:A Bradford Book, the MIT Press.

McGaugh, J. L. (1995) Emotional activation, neuromodulatory systems, and memory. In D.Schachter (Ed.) *Memory Distortion: How Minds, Brains, and Societies Reconstruct the Past.* U.S.A.: The President and Fellows of Harvard University.

Miller, G, A. (1956) The magical number seven, plus or minus two: Some limits on our capacity for processing information. *Psychological Review*, 63, 81-97.

Milojkovic, J. D. and Ross, L. (1981) Telling truths from lies: miscalibration of confidence and base-rate utilization. *Paper presented at the American Psychological Association.*

Olson, P.L. (1996) *Forensic Aspects of Driver Perception and Response.* Tucson, AZ. Lawyers & Judges Publishing Company, Inc.

Olson, P.L. and Farber, E. (2003) *Forensic Aspects of Driver Perception and Response, Second Edition.* Tucson, AZ. Lawyers & Judges Publishing Company, Inc.

Schacter, D.L. (1995) *Memory Distortion: How Minds, Brains, and Societies Reconstruct the Past.* U.S.A.: The President and Fellows of Harvard University.

Simons, Daniel J. And Chabris, Christopher F. (1999) Gorillas in our midst: sustained inattentional blindness for dynamic events. *Perception*, Volume 28, pp.1059-1074.

Sperling, G. (1960) The information available in brief visual presentations. *Psychological Monographs*, 74, 1-29.

Squire, L. R. (1995) Biological foundations of accuracy and inaccuracy in memory. In D.Schachter (Ed.) *Memory Distortion: How Minds, Brains, and Societies Reconstruct the Past.* U.S.A.: The President and Fellows of Harvard University.

Weingartner, H., Miller, H., Murphy, D.L. (1977). Mood-state dependent retrieval of verbal associations. *Journal of Abnormal Psychology* 86: 276-284.

Yerkes, R.M. and Dodson, J.D. (1908) The relation of strength of stimulus to rapidity of habit-formation. *Journal of Comparative and Neurological Psychology* 18: 459-482.

About the Author

Patrick J. Robins received a Ph.D. in Social/Industrial Psychology from the University of Manitoba in 1983 and began a teaching career in the Department of Psychology at Ryerson Polytechnic University in Toronto, Canada that same year. In 1988, he joined Ryerson's newly founded Vehicle Safety Research Centre, one of eight multi-disciplinary university- based teams in Canada contracted by Transport Canada to provide national motor vehicle accident and defect investigations. He was the Senior Collision Investigator and Team Manager when he left the Ryerson Team in 1997 to devote his full attention to his collision reconstruction business in Toronto. His company, Virtual Crash Animation and Reconstruction, provides consultation on a variety of traffic crash reconstruction issues, including human factors.

Dr. Robins has regularly taught crash reconstruction courses including human factors training for the University of North Florida's Institute of Police Technology and Management as well as both the Canadian Police College and the Ontario Provincial Police College. He is a member of the Canadian Association of Technical Accident Investigators and Reconstructionists (CATAIR) and the Human Factors and Ergonomics Society (HFES).

Index

Breinigsville, PA USA
29 September 2010
246356BV00001B/10/P